AN ANTHOLOGY OF IM

POETRY
for the
PLANET

Edited by

Julia Kaylock and Denise O'Hagan

LITORIA PRESS

First published 2021
by Litoria Press, Victoria, Australia
+61 3 59852112
litoriapress@gmail.com
www.litoriapress.com

ISBN 978-0-6451145-7-7 (p/back)
978-0-6451145-8-4 (ebook)

NATIONAL LIBRARY OF AUSTRALIA
A catalogue record for this work is available from the National Library of Australia

Cover design by Julia Kaylock and Brendan Bonsack
Front cover image: Blue Spring Te Waihou Walkway, near Putāruru, NZ, (IStock: momo11353)
Back cover image: Global Warming (IStock: gan chaonan)

Printed and bound in Australia.

Commendations

'If poetry is not for the planet, it's hard, these days, to know what on earth poetry *is* for. Manifestly, poetry cannot save the earth or slow, by itself, the collapse of ecosystems, or cool the coming age of fire; but there is no hope without poetry. For poetry can—by virtue of its lyric gift for getting said what is felt and known but is otherwise unsayable—conserve in us what may just stir us to conserve what remains of the wild and habitable earth.

'For two hundred years, and more than ever today, our discourses have forgotten—have denied—the earth. Literature, in its forgetfulness of more-than-merely human narratives, has been complicit in bringing on the Anthropocene, the climate catastrophe we face. The lyric, though, is earth's idiom; poetry is the planet's first (human) language. Only poetry is adequate for what earth does and how it suffers—and for the plumbing of human natures upon the planet. In the poetry of all cultures in all ages, nature has been divined and its wreck decried. Some poetry, of course, tracking the anthropocentric and exploitive trajectories of dominant cultures, has failed the earth and us upon it—but most has not.

'And in these poems, tenderly curated by Julia Kaylock and Denise O'Hagan, earth is well and wisely remembered and a diminished future is starkly earth adumbrated—in case there may still be time for the waking of our minds and the firing of our spirits upon which all our futures on the planet depend. There is an urgency in these poems; there is tenderness, too. There are many fine poets here, old and young, from many continents, and there are poems in many forms and voices and moods and attitudes, from rage to grief to resignation—here is an open forest of phrase, a garden in a city; here the kind of diversity upon which all thriving depends.

' "How long does it take not to see something again?" asks David Brooks. Here is a book of poems to help us see again: what we have done, what we have forgotten to delight in, what we might yet do.'

Mark Tredinnick, poet and essayist

'This generous anthology presents poetry steeped in a fierce love of the natural world, combined with a tragic sense of our human failing to cherish and protect it. Desolate futures are imagined: "Finally we're all reduced/to passengers in steerage/on this titanic earth/gradually sinking." However, more importantly, the art of the poet makes us see wonder and beauty with fresh eyes, particularly in the otherness of nature, and challenges us to save what we can, while we can. As another poet intimates, it's "Time for us/to be a sea of change." These poems compellingly show us why.'

Patricia Gemmell

'The cost of nonchalance: "Who'll bookmark a future / that happened yesterday?" asks Anne Elvey in 'A climate of mortality meets Melbourne winter.' At a time when the Intergovernmental Panel on Climate Change has just released the first instalment of its landmark Sixth Assessment Report, this moving anthology of poems from Australia and New Zealand could not be more topical. *Poetry for the Planet* reminds us how human beings are suffocating the biosphere and its life. Two opening poems by the editors prelude an astonishing collection of work exploring the cost of our nonchalance, lamenting what is lost, yet holding hope in its pages. A thought-provoking book for everyone, particularly the politicians who have betrayed us for so long.'

Hazel Hall, poet and musicologist

'*Poetry for the Planet* is the anthology the world needs right now. This collection of poems has been perfectly collated and curated to ensure the reader can open up to any page and find words that resonate, that heal, that challenge and that light a fire within, to leave this planet in a better place.'

Niel Smith, Perth poet

Foreword

Australia and New Zealand are home to some of the most amazing wildlife, places and people on the planet. Our incredible natural world defines us, unites us and inspires us to do everything we can to protect our planet—for all living things.

This love of our planet, the grief for life that has already been destroyed, the fear of the darkness ahead, and the courage to decide to make a difference is evident in the poems you are about to read.

I was moved by the deep connection the poets have with people and nature and the plants and animals they observe. I was struck by the sense of devastation surrounding what is under threat and the loss driven by climate-fuelled bushfires, droughts and floods.

We cannot shy away from the grim reality we face. Things are not as they should be.

But we must also inspire action. We must lean into hope and solutions in our storytelling, to raise the energy within and drive momentum to protect and revitalise our forests, rivers, oceans—and the incredible plants and animals that call them home.

Activist and author Rebecca Solnit tells us the future may be dark, but it is not set. If we can imagine a better future, we can inspire people to get to work and create it.

That's why poems are so important. They have the power to stir emotions, offer new perspectives and unite ideas. There is no single way to share messages of our climate and extinction crises. And the more ways our communities can be moved by what is at stake, the more people will speak up and demand action.

And we've never needed greater action than we do now.

Australia is a world leader in extinctions. Nearly 2000 Australian plants, animals and ecosystems are currently threatened with extinction, and these are just the ones we know about.

New Zealand has the highest proportion of threatened indigenous species in the world.

For nations renowned for our magnificent nature, we don't treat her very well.

The number one cause of extinction is habitat destruction—from logging, mining, urban sprawl and bushfires supercharged by climate change. Many species we may think of as common, like the koala, kiwi and platypus, are being hit hard by this combination of threats.

And then, the knockout punch of climate change looms. People around the world were heartbroken by the news that around three billion animals were killed or displaced by the Australian bushfires. It's not just the sheer numbers but the long-term—in some cases permanent—damage to unique ecosystems that is so concerning.

In a climate that is warmer, wetter and more energetic, we're seeing increasing fires, storms, flooding and disruption to life. But while the eco-anxiety can feel immense and overwhelming for many of us, I firmly believe our future—and our present—is one of resilience and change.

This is the moment when we must 'get emotional about climate change', as social researcher Dr Rebecca Huntly says; the time when we should be moved to talk creatively about what's at stake and what we can do about it.

It's also a time when we can revitalise our communities with projects and industries that are good for people, for our climate, for nature, and for our future. We can never stop asking for the change we want.

These motivations can carry us into the future and allow us to re-imagine what's possible. To be resilient and to thrive, we can remind ourselves of the good and the beauty in the world. And there is so much beauty to reflect on, not only in nature, but in the generosity, humour, kindness and care of our communities who keep coming up with creative actions to help solve these problems.

More frequently, we are being told action on climate change is a divisive issue. But the real story on climate change has never been (nor should be) about pitting city against country, producers against consumers, environment against business.

It's about finding our common ground: working together with people from all walks of life, and, importantly, being guided by First Nations peoples who hold unique knowledge and rights inherited from their ancestors and Country, and who have cared for our countries since time immemorial.

The way forward will be joyful, sad, surprising and frustrating. We'll experience great leaps forward and devastating setbacks. We've encountered all these before.

As advocates, we seek to change the world and sometimes that can seem impossible. But it's not. We just need to remember that this is 'the beginning, not the end', and what might seem impossible is just going to take some time.

Kelly O'Shanassy
Chief Executive Officer
Australian Conservation Foundation

Contents

A LENS ON BIODIVERSITY

A LIKELY HABITAT

INSCRIBING OUR DESTINY

About the editors

Julia Kaylock lives on BoonWurrung/ Bunurong Country. She has poetry and prose published in journals and anthologies including *The Blue Nib* (Issue 41, 2020), *Live Encounters* (May 2021), *Grieve* Volume 8 (Hunter Writers Centre, 2020) and *Globalisation* (MMH Press, 2021). In 2020, Julia co-edited *Messages from the Embers: From Devastation to Hope* (Black Quill Press).

In late 2020 Julia launched her own publishing company, with several titles already published. In August 2021, she released her memoir, *Child of the Clouds: A Memoir in Verse about Adoption Trauma and Recovery* litoriapress.com. Find Julia's poetry at juliakaylock.com

Denise O'Hagan is an editor and poet, based in Sydney. She has a background in commercial book publishing with Collins, Routledge and Heinemann (London) and Harcourt Brace Jovanovich, Horwitz Educational, and the State Library of NSW (Sydney). In 2015, she set up her own imprint, Black Quill Press, through which she assists independent authors.

Denise's poetry is published widely and has received numerous awards, most recently the Dalkey Poetry Prize 2020. Her debut poetry collection is *The Beating Heart* (Ginninderra Press, 2020).
https://denise-ohagan.com

Dedication and acknowledgments

This anthology is dedicated to Planet Earth and all creatures that live on her.

In the spirit of reconciliation, on behalf of all who appear in this work, Litoria Press acknowledges the Traditional Custodians of Country throughout Australia and their connections to land, sea and community. We pay our respect to their elders past and present and extend that respect to all Aboriginal and Torres Strait Islander peoples.

Additionally, we affirm and acknowledge Māori as the tangata whenua (indigenous people) and kaitiaki (guardians) of Aotearoa New Zealand.

We acknowledge the work of climate change and biodiversity trailblazers including Dr Jane Goodall, Sir David Attenborough and Greta Thunberg, and hope that these poems go beyond being 'beautiful words'* to reach into the hearts and minds of those who read, and encourage positive action.

*used in Greta's speech at the Austrian World Summit, 1 July 2021

Net profits from sales go to the Australian Conservation Foundation

With thanks

We extend our heartfelt thanks to all who assisted us in bringing this anthology to life: all the poets from Australia and New Zealand who submitted work so generously, and especially Amanda Anastasi for her support of us in myriad ways including kindly supplying the monostich poems which introduce each of the parts.

Many thanks also to Brendan Bonsack for dealing with many changes of mind and about-facing during the process of creating the cover. From the positive feedback we have received, it was worth it!

To all who purchase a copy, on behalf of the Australian Conservation Foundation, we thank you enormously.

Introduction

Whilst receiving submissions for *Messages from the Embers: From Devastation to Hope* (Black Quill Press, October 2020), we realised that poets were attuned to broader issues impacting (often negatively) the future for all species. This gave rise to *Poetry for the Planet: An Anthology of Imagined Futures*, to encourage poets living in Australia and New Zealand to further contemplate and explore these issues.

As poets, we like to consider ourselves as conveyors of truths; our aim, to crystallise thoughts and ideas through new narratives: 'imagining futures', if you like. Of course, poetry can hardly save the planet, on its own anyway, so one may wonder if this kind of endeavour is worth the effort. Are we 'fiddling while Rome burns'? Are we simply procrastinating, or even adding a few more nails to Earth's coffin? Should we not be doing something practical instead, to save the planet? Or, can poets make a difference to perceptions about the big issues, and consequently affect how we live our lives?

The rise in ecopoetry is testament to how seriously poets view the current ecological crisis: poetic imagination inspired close to 500 submissions for this project alone. Our aim has been to add many voices to an urgent conversation on matters of climate change, the environment, impacts on biodiversity and, especially, the way human activity is influencing all of these. It is a delight to include both established and emerging poets in what we hope will become a pivotal artefact in the move towards positive change for our planet.

The poems were organised into four parts to form a narrative, highlighting the central themes.

Please enjoy reading this anthology, and thank you for supporting the work done by the Australian Conservation Foundation.

Julia and Denise

Ficus macrophylla

Denise O'Hagan

It was a spur-of-the-moment backward glance
But for a moment it was all I saw—
A gigantic sprawling metaphor
Blotting out the pale blue sky
Stretching upwards and out
Through olive-green drapery
Across a rustling of generations
Towards sun and sea
To the here and now.

The flesh of its trunk
Swollen with years
Sprouts drooping roots
Great locks of knotted greying hair
Moving heavily with the breeze
And mottled, lengthy, hefty arms
A tangle of whorls and curves and elbows
Rounded and hollowed with time and rain,
Hold up a vast weight, and our dreams.

And so this *Ficus macrophylla*
Matronly and majestic in equal measure
Rises above its solemn Latin label
(attached long ago by earnest botanists)
Doesn't give a fig for it or any other word
As it speaks another language
That of century-old fortitude
Stillness, and succour.

A medusozoan planet

Julia Kaylock

The seas that surround the land are rising...
the land is under threat like never before in human existence.
—Simon Winchester, *Land* (HarperCollins, 2021)

increasingly large jellyfish aggregations are indicators of declining health of the world's oceans
—Lisa-Ann Gershwin, *Stung!* (University of Chicago Press, 2013)

Coastlines wither,
careless waves envelop abandoned seafront mansions,
—no money changes hands in this land grab.
Sandbags, unwilling accomplices to vain coveters of things,
once valiantly surrounded a contrived habitat;
now emptied, rinsed and relegated by the ocean,
in its empty-nesting grief-hoarder
stage of life,
to the epipelagic museum of interesting artefacts.

The humans are long gone, yet evidence of their existence
is persuasive:
unprecedented, a new being will inscribe,
in a garret far away
prevaricating on possibilities for 'Once upon a time'.

but that's a story for the future, after the revelation.
In our 'now', we fight a useless war against everything,
taming, draining, reclaiming;
dark-minded we plunder,
wildly surmising supremacy status

while, regardless of our inclination for debating issues,
philosophising, categorising—
temperatures rise, icecaps melt, seas swell;
whilst in our blind spot,
bright colonies of bioluminescence
await the call:
nematocyst-assisted extinction,
recording the last shining moments
of the hunger—

it's doom-by-design,
an all-inclusive package
from the species with a yen
for self-destruction.

COUNTRY—A CAUTIONARY TALE

'The ocean is holding the weight of our apathy.'

Amanda Anastasi

'interest is payable from the start of destruction.'

—Earth in voice, *Margaret Owen Ruckert*

'The river stretches out its fingers, to where it used to hug the darkness with its life.'

—The Carmichael Mine, *Emily Mitchell*

'Alas! The earth, mad with thirst,
devoured the last of our water.'

—Giant Barramundi, *Matina Doumos*

'I do not want to meet this vanishing.'

—the glaciers, *Gillian Swain*

Greenshrink

The car peeps over the hill.
As my eyebrows rise to match
the knolls we slalom
the kids chorus
enjoy the view while you can.

We thread the aching paddocks,
granted and taken
peeled and shrunk.
The kids roll their eyes
my grief so predictable.

But I know each time will
be the last I see of this sweep of
hill and sky.
Each new drive trips the senses,
curbs and guttering cut a way
to new vacancies.

Each hill a wing
arced across hard-packed
silence.

Gillian Swain

Earth tessellates

The earth tessellates, still at times soft in the belly
But already cracks harden, open, widen
Mouthing at sky. You can hardly tell it's a lake here
—at least the map says so—
layering blue across parched soil.
The cartographers should have used brown crosshatching
Thrown up their arms at vacillating boundaries
(which are just a river now—more a creek)
Exposing rocks with threading quartz seams
Which we toss into stilling pools
That play at being lakes, as water splashes skyward
Shedding small tsunamis to the brittle-edged shore.

Carl Walsh

Haiku

Beauty of nature
Orange skies—
If only we did not know

Edna Heled

sanctity of shadows
wildlife regenerates
in leafy vestibule

Dianne Cikusa

Once wild pristine stream.
Mine tunnels. Sandstone bed cracks
Toxic soup stagnates.

Leigh Roswen

Point Lookout

Berarngutta, meaning 'prohibited area', a men-only site

Flesh drips from a static dance scarved in lichen, matted
in moss. Competition for space is covert but intense,
decomposition rapid but discrete. Filaments of fungi

embroider fashionable fabrics cabbage-green or pale
fructose—'canaries', crusty, fibrous, forked or folded lichens,
symbiotic alliances sensitive to pollution and climate change.

Pertusaria slaps molten silver onto snow gums, orchids
clamber over fallen felted trees melting beneath a tapestry
pinned with liverworts surfacing as trompe-l'oeil doilies.

We track the edge of this Gondwana remnant, a dilapidated
installation, abstracted architecture. The world is white,
the eastern yellow robin taking wing appears almost grey.

Even on the brink the horizon is missing and was never ours.
Dunghutti tales, homeless too long are being retold, they fought
'the history wars' and now fight for the past to curate the present.

The nearest ridge scrawls Antarctic beech on a blurred prow,
Antarctica is melting and tainted, so this air must be wrong
and tears leaves salvaged from the mist. Is entropy accelerating?

I chat to two botanists from Mount Annan's plant bank,
here to fossick for new flowers and detect discrepancies.
I said, 'if you ask me', (poets rarely are, at Plato's request)

'it's like captive breeding programs, or de-extinction fantasies.
What's the bloody point if habitat is trashed?' And they agreed.
It's weird but the world no longer belongs to itself.

John Bennett

At sea

Brine rises, whetted as memories in my sandbagged lungs—
plastic-scrap semi-sunk in a spring tide, ragged and limp, as hard to inflate.

I came from the sea, a distant shore pummelled even then—
beaches these days reshaped by each season, squalls outside living recollection.

Seawater pillowed my children before they were born—
blood-warm as the currents swarming to nurture the crown of thorns, they thrived into life.

Wave-surges swell on the storm-ravaged islands of my consciousness—
welling like water-winged infants, as vulnerable to submersion; I still worry they'll drown.

My body grows nodules virulent as invaders engulfing virile organs—
once plump and vigorous as coral polyps, my cells too, pulse with petrochemicals.

My temperature rises with each falling number—
two thousand species, two thousand metres deep, two thousand kilometres wide.

My heart sinks—
faster than the five hundred billion plastic bags we use each year.

My vision clouds—
murky as forty per cent of the world's ocean surface obscured in
manmade debris.

But, small and bright as spawn-clouds blooming—
white, gold, coral, the young surfacing, shine through seeking truth,

our budding hope

Anne Casey

Public health warning

'no swimming or shellfish collecting'

Two white ducks
ignore this edict
and arise from
the condemned stream
shaking their wings
fetid drops sparkling.

Piers Davies

ecstatic dance

or, *Nude on the River*

murray, darling, look at me
I've lost your reflection
no narcissus in this steel gauze
and I am dancing your return
one foot, then two, the instep
a cautious depth into my own skin
I am scared of you as you kiss
my white-faced heron toes
and the sun a kiln a candle asks
to take you for its own
what *pas de deux* can coax
your calm return? what song
do the fish sing? I would sing it
if I knew, if you spoke to me,
murray, darling, do not
leave me like this

Claire Albrecht

A hill outside Yanchep

A swell in the geography
is a lower jaw
five months after
a punch in the face.

Blackened tooth stumps;
scatter, evidence,
on the vanished border
once named 'tree line.'

Pig-tail smoke curls
exhale between grains;
black dirt burnt white;
breath of yesterday's visitor.

The quiet is roaring, wheezing,
dreaming of methane.
Ruthless silence,
in the days after birdsong

Alan Fyfe

The Carmichael mine

Fifty years from now, a small town perches on the edge of a monstrous cavern. Look around, and see what we created: in the earth, a resounding abyss, a gaping grave, thousands of metres wide. The land is wailing, it is in mourning for the country has been gouged away, and where it stood in all its splendour, trucks roar past and trudge its glory into dust.

Along the horizon—which would have been marked by feathered hills, emerald-green farmland, scrubby grasses, red dirt rich in resonance, wild colour, lines and shadow, tall white eucalypts that have weathered wild storms and the overthrowing of governments—yawns a cavern that jerks, jostles and hurtles in the dark with black stone. The birds feel it under their feet far away and the river aches as it is pummelled by constant sound and demolition.

The river stretches out its fingers, to where it used to hug the darkness with its life, and speaks:

you and i are being separated,
but you will come back to me and poison me

On the reef, the coral is bright with agitation—neon blue, iridescent purple, it is sending out its last buds of life, its emergency signal to reproduce, recreate, regenerate, but its arms are too heavy and hot to hold its magnificence any longer; and it shrinks and fades.

Marine villages of coral: suburbs, railways, community centres, fish highways, become silent and still in the warm, warm water. The coral stretches out its arms, to where it used to hug the ocean with its life, and speaks:

i thought you and i would never be separated
but i will crumble and become the dirty sand at your feet
and where fish sang and starfish dreamed
and shells crept and anemones wept
there will be silence

And the guardians stand at the gate outside, Wangan and Jagalingou. And with the mantle of millennia they speak:

We are the Country and the Country is Us
We can never be separated.

In parliaments in decades to come, they will hold inquiries examining how this came to pass—how our chronic myopia choked the future, our focus became so clouded, so errored with judgement. And a committee will make a small recommendation in fine print that means nothing.

And in countries far away, men count their money with fat eyes, list figures and statistics with glossed cheeks and eat and drink to their heart's content and excess, in finery, in beautiful houses and estates on mountains that will never be carved up. And they lick their fingers as they eat in a cool air-conditioned room.

Emily Mitchell

Adani's Carmichael mine is destined to be one of the largest coal mines in the world. The Wangan and Jagalingou people, the land's traditional owners and custodians, have consistently opposed the mine on their ancestral lands.

the glaciers

I don't want to see the glaciers
I can't sit on their cracked lips
feel mother earth lick the waiting

the slip
no time to return
welcome cold

I can't visit their loss
shared grief
would drown me

nakedness skins the rising
I cannot trace their drier eyes
my steps would fill them with new tears

I would hear the crack
sing sharp through hearts of centuries

I do not want to meet this vanishing

Gillian Swain

Confusion in my garden

Christmas lilies in May
Untimely display of elegance
in soft cream and blush pink
Outwitting the Vireyas
Not yet ready to compete
Their hidden orange blooms
Still tightly encased.
Lilies face up to the sun
Beautiful in 'so there' defiance
Distracting us from the message
In this clement, genial display.
Out of time
Out of order.
The warmth thickens in the still air
As we tilt dangerously away from our familiar seasons.

Helen Anderson

Reflections

Waves lick at basalt
fringing the intertidal reef
as hooded plovers scoot the shore,
red-rimmed eyes, legs a-blur.
A girl weaves through sastrugi on the sand.

Waves lick at bones
of homes eroded,
as sandbags hold a futile front
against the rising tide.
A girl darts furtively across the scalding sand.

Pastel skies reflected on the glassy shallows
start to tremble, as her
tentative toe
tests the surface tension.
Blennies dart below billowing seaweed.

Smoky skies reflected on the stagnant shallows
start to warp, as her
tentative toe
tests the surface slick.
Armies of urchins invade the barracks below.

Her surfboard sends out sinusoids;
water beads on wax.
Her hands stroke forth
in syncopation,
pulling at the deepening emerald sea.

Her surfboard dodges flotsam;
knotted nylon drags behind.
Her hands stroke forth
in desperation
parting plastic debris for the deep.

The pulse of a virile ocean
beats out a steady
peak and trough.
She rides her board in tempo,
thrust forward in a symbiotic dance.

The pulse of a febrile ocean
beats in unsteady
fibrillation.
She yields herself, as acid
waves unleash the rage

of an unbalanced world.

Helena Baird

The fall

after Arthur Boyd's *Nebuchadnezzar on fire falling over a waterfall*

In the upper course of the river
Where the mountains are steep
The hooked trees are thick with
Their feathery presence and after
Rain there is a lushness, a rush
And a plunge to the punchbowl
Below

My foot caught the sun—I flew
Too high and their yellow eyes,
The colour of the fire sky touched
Turquoise, magenta, watch me oxidise
At daybreak—limbs white hot and
Cascading ash

So I wish I'd listened. There, I said
It. I wish I could gulp time with
Flame and breathe back peace
But they say nothing now—heads
Bowed, wings close by their sides
At the tops of the deathly pale
Trees

Nothing will change. There will be
Endless fires and storms and the
Sky will turn red and the waterfalls
Will run dry. There will be kinetic
Cold and this madness of my own
Making will end. People have
Climates too
I will fall

Jane Frank

River of time

The currents swirling
summer, autumn, winter, spring
in circles of time
each ending a beginning
each droplet flowing in life
that river of time
old Heraclitus once viewed
has since been bottled
sold for travel in vessels
like HG Wells' machine
denying the truth
time travel is possible
if you will believe
watch a river and observe
droplets will fly across streams
landing far away
as the lazy waters
flow downhill
to the sea
read a map and you will see
rivers can move over time
they leave impressions
abandon tributaries
follow gravity
unchecked flows swamp foundations
stranding elevated knobs
those rocky outlooks
isolated and distant

clutching onto land
John Donne lied about islands
streams will divide
continents ideas will find
flows punctuated by contrasts
where dated views hold
after water pools and calms
welcome the bridge of friendship
find ground to stand on
hold your head above water
know islands will form
time travel is possible
just don't become lost in time
make your way through cracks
become like water my friend
learn to be fluid

Jason Richardson

The estuary, Valla NSW

Gyrating on dawn's inkling, the size of an eastern
bentwing bat circles like a ragged butterfly overhead

then flips into the canopy. I settle on emerging colours.
The herons are alert rock-angel silhouettes,

silver gulls mob a brahminy kite, blank grey this early.
The sea is bouncing onto the beach, flurries of wave

punch through the teeth, but the water settles
to pool the precious lumens. Fish are jumping.

At yesterday's opening Andrew mentioned he was here
last week and amazed how many fish there were.

I ask if fish jump to escape predators or to catch prey?
I googled once but don't recall a persuasive answer.

He is a fish expert, renowned artist and a Buddhist.
He smiled, 'they do it for the joy'.

Patterns of flow, curves, loops, interference patterns
and the circular ripples fish spark are mandalas

evoking the Tao. The sun is pushing clouds apart,
Pied and sooty oystercatchers, head down, probe territory.

Heading upriver I turn a corner into a juvenile osprey
which banks abruptly and soars up into the opening sky.

I stand chanting on the breath, little black cormorants
arrive a little late towing an angel-white egret.

I could conjugate this estuary, it almost looks
as if things have stayed the same for ever.

John Bennett

Wilderness, untouched

A canopy quivering with foliage

snakes through our fantasies
Hidden gullies, pockets of primeval ferns.

Shut your eyes to see it.

Antediluvian forests, waterfalls
cresting off unclimbed mountain peaks.

Rivers, silver-thick with salmon.

The fragrance of damp pine
and swamp gums unremarked upon.

A labyrinth of caves, virgin hollows
never illuminated or mapped.

Still and empty as the desert. Not even a whimper
of human restlessness or discontent.

Birds in bright plumage, their mating calls

unrecorded. Blossoms unplucked.
No reference in sketches or love poems.

Plant specimens never pressed
between glass slides and shipped for cataloguing.

Red earth, unsown, unharvested.
No mumbled prayer,
just the wind's sharp intake of awe.

Nights alive with fur creatures foraging,
unacquainted with bullets and traps.

Perhaps frogs, the size of fingernails

in primary colours. Blue-tongued lizards.
Moths and butterflies forever nameless.

Alluvial soils, crystals—even gold.
Somewhere— fiery blooms and untasted fruit.

But without a witness, how can we be sure?

Laura Jan Shore

A pelican on Lake Eyre

Did she follow the first waters
as they snaked along a dusty
Channel Country riverbed
like a lonely drover trailing
sheep in the long paddock.

Did she notice a tropical storm
wash down from the Kimberley
spattering raindrops on the desert
sand the way goanna footprints
sweep across a bark painting.

Was she in the Top End watching
cloud head south with its load
as heavy as a morning catch
about to be slung onto the cold, steel
deck of an expectant trawler.

Did the local finches, having drunk
from the newly filled saltpans,
pass the news, beak to beak
over the bush telegraph until it reached
a broody pelican in the Coorong.

And having found this inland paradise,
will her unsuspecting chick learn to fly
or will its partly feathered carcass
lie wasted in the drying mud, one eye
pointed toward an unrepentant sun.

Gregory Piko

Good Earth

Weereewa/Lake George

after i've stopped, please
throw the burnt bits of all
of me into whatever
winds are flying
over the open plains
in this place of vanishing

Matt Hetherington

Beeliar

A wetland, liminal
not fully sand nor water
not a steady or marketable quality,
but rich; an open ground of dialogue,
changing needs and shift—
now ten percent of what we had
drying-up in the sift of history.
Words and lakes, lost
amidst clay bricks and market gardens,
rubbish tips, quarries and parkland.
Whole knowings lopped in this glut.
To re-conjure these brackish landscapes
reach through the silt and slough
to that nipple:
          braille of place.

Sunny Wignall

Summer ice

It's thought to have been there
for sixteen million years
but who knows now,
maybe twenty, maybe ten more.

You imagine polar bears,
so soft and savage,
clinging to their icy rafts.

This long ride seems to be ending.
Luxurious for some,
wretched for most.

Finally we're all reduced
to passengers in steerage
on this titanic earth
gradually sinking.

Mark Mahemoff

Mortal enemies

Our rainforests cling
desperate and liminal
on the edges of desiccated land
shyly in valleys they shelter then morph
in ecotonal zones below south-facing cliffs
where soft and hard leafed trees hide together
from the worst predators known to nature.

We are too clever for our own
—or the planet's—good
the masterful conquest of 'our *domaine*'
means we move mountains—
dream of travel to other worlds yet ignore
we are just another chain of carbon
on the same Earth that fossil fools wrap
in a terracidal electric blanket.

Shakespeare could have written
the tragedy of our kind
where what makes us exceptional also ruins us
but perhaps, we are more the stuff of comedy
being wilfully obtuse.

Each action our growth economies take
seems only to make the climate hotter, drier
allow Gondwana species to vaporise
never consider *The Spirit of the Plains*
and deny what it *is* happening

here and now, under well-heeled feet
in plundered dirt or in red dust
which storms the emerald city.

Along the ranges that landlock the urban sprawl
the legendary blue haze fades
to a granite grey of mourning
as charred black trunks are made fuzzy
by bright green shoots
as lignotubers standby—
ready for the sclerophyll march.

Linda Adair

The Spirit of the Plains is a painting by Sydney Long

The Baaka brolgas

We walked the memory of water
on our step and stumble pilgrimage.
Moving silently over ancient rocks
    we wound
            our
              way
                 along
                      the weary riverbed
bearing witness to the salty tidemarks
of greed and ignorance.
River red-gums sought lifelines
in the bosom of the darling Baaka:
fragile progeny suckling for moisture
—tenuous respite.
Ragged
     heaps
           of
              feathered
                    bone
marked   out   time
and loss of country’s disappearing brolgas.
He said his people spoke with brolgas
that used to come and visit in the autumn:
they told his people stories
that needed to be heard.

He talked his memories
of these silky plumaged kin:
of how they shook shimmer-dancing
across ephemeral swamps
their joyful leaping
through lush flooded grasslands
nestling chicks in silver water
dipping soft red-orange heads
towards each other
towards flocks of hopeful swans
winging north to meet fresh water
—that might not come.
His darling Baaka's quiet now
hushed as the black-tipped wings
of threatened brolgas.
His people's story-times of water
and of brolgas
now recalled in tears.

Lorraine Gibson

The Baaka forms part of the longest river system in Australia and is part of Indigenous Barkindji country. Barkindji means *'belonging to the river'*.

Non-Indigenous people know The Baaka as *The Darling River.*
For my friend and Barkindji Elder Badger Bates.

Earth in voice

This is not an invoice in the strictest terms
but a final demand. Non-negotiable and now.
No voice is too loud for your in-tray pile.

I never said sell. I was never the goods
    but somehow, from under my reserves of wellness
    you slunk in, tractor-foot, sullen-stare
    ripped me open, never-care, try and deny it
    abused the unknowable, torched and ran
    slashed the priceless forest mantle
    plundered my worth to worthless and less.
What on earth powers your commonsense?

What special event could be more valued
than keeping alive the work of time?
If money terms are all you've learnt
upskill now with this poetic note:
    interest is payable from the start of destruction
    and compounds daily on my instructions
    and isn't it comforting to now explore
    how ignorance is no part of law
    you haven't got a credit on any of my days
    I've never seen a signature that stayed the same.

You owe me everything you've taken and more.
Shall we try an inventory before you excuse
tomorrow's profit on *your* exemplary skills:

you owe me air without disclaimers
you owe me water and everyone else
you owe me landscape, wildlife, the works.

You war with yourselves and think I don't notice.
Restore my ray shield before we're a burn out.
And don't think intelligence is strictly humanoid.
My insects learn a little faster than you.
I don't take dirt money; I just take pure dirt.
You owe it all back and it's payable now.

Man, make those commitments
PAYABLE: TO EARTH
and also be warned
I plan to hang round.

Margaret Owen Ruckert

On snow gums

granite ridge
blue gums give way
to snow gums

boulder-hopping
to the summit
snow gums

mountain campsite
between the snow gums
stars

chasing moonlight
a twisting path
of snow gums

snow gums
our breath mingles
with clouds

the tangled branches
of burnt snow gums
magpie song

a long ridge
of charred snow gums
silver clouds

Louise Hopewell

the layering

all week
they have flown east
sad slow flight.
dust and history
deep in feather
sing old words

sky reflects country
water reflects sky

we have watched
ice embers dust
float onto soil
a story reading
winds currents
history layering
onto a recent garden

country never becomes used to these blasts
Mamu riding a mushroom cloud
a musket shot piecing the *Gweagal Shield*

each of us in isolation
senses the splintering the loss
culture reduced to dust

Mark Roberts

Response to the latest global warming statistics

Raindrops we collect fall through our fingers
to footpaths for sparrows. they take off

their beaks in appreciation,
bend & peck the shadows.

What we and the birds refuse to recall
comes back to haunt us: first as a ghost

in a child's ghost costume
then fully grown in sheets of hail.

Frightened, all the mirrors we own walk from our houses
and jump in the murky river.

(We finally see ourselves clearly
and our waterway. So humane.)

There is cause for celebration.
There are causes for everything.
Except first causes. And that breadcrumbs us back

to missing raindrops
and sparrows. They put their beaks back on,

don simple suits and tell us
not one of them falls from the sky
without forward planning. We ignore them,

listen for trees falling in forests
ten thousand Saturn moons away.
We fail to count the rings but the wind

at last stops howling.
We set up our white cloth dinner table
on the mountaintop. Empty plates the waiters

spin on fingers
are entertaining. So are the melting
glaciers and

when the sun finally finishes dying
we gather at the crematorium
to watch distant stars shine like ice cubes.

Paul Mitchell

Giant barramundi

The dreams of old finally withered
by this blighted watering hole.
Having no blood of their own
for years we infused them with ours,
but flourish they would not
grafted on our foreign flesh.

So we let them die, those dreams
which had sucked us dry,
and we mated in desperation
longing for a dream of our own,
with clear autistic eyes
fixed upon the horizon;

a god we too could worship.
Alas! The earth, mad with thirst,
devoured the last of our water,
and subtle poisons leaching
from the old dream roots
soon thwarted our hopes;

left us clinging to each other
sunk to our torsos in clay.
But at night we sense songlines
throbbing overhead, we cast for
giant barramundi, maroons
of another alien Dreaming.

Matina Doumos

In conversation with Brian

Brian Turner said it best and I wonder
are there words to say it otherwise
and yet—when you are faced with

earth scooped clean, as if around
the corner and out-of-sight is a
waffle cone, caramel choc chip,
and silvered trails of liquid light
and a smear of blueblueblue
and a mist-down blanket
            steals your breath

and then, *Aoraki*

presses my heart to iced gravel
at the viewing point where the
promised glacier cannot be seen
but you can hear its rumbling call, retreat
to the mountain top
where the whole mess is laid out fresh
droughtpandemicgreedfloodsmoke

And there at the poetry workshop, Brian
beseeching us to find the words, to hold
the weight of them close

Rachel Smith

Seven sijo in July

I got back before nightfall,
but the day kept going on and on into the present.
—Philip Levine

May the past be merciful, the landscape have pity on me—
Forgive me my words, forgive me my utterances.
—Charles Wright

I
White-grey frost on the tip of morning—silence, except rosellas
Finding their place in it all. I'm not alone, this house of lovers
Throws itself into the winter sky.
I breath, daily repentance.

II
The canna lilies have forgotten, the sun cools early July;
The day thaws in puddles. At noon, a lawnmower finds its calling,
The little raven reminds me too
—the damp earth is full of bounty.

III
The wind is all I hear today; the plum tree a poor conductor
In the sky, clouds keep the rhythm, a kestrel spread its wings like a kite
Then cymbals crash in the tussock
grass—he beats the air, mouse in claw.

IV
Paddocks' dry; cattle egret, white-necked heron, pied cormorant.
The dam shrinks from its duty—winter fallen on the highlands.
I am home, swaddled in your hand,
                                        both tears and rain are a gift.

V
In Robertson, fog is the earth's muse   these late July afternoons,
Cows ascend a bare hillside;   mountain grey gum on the east fringe.
Clarity, in the dew damp grass
                                        —water droplets hold the sun.

VI
Macquarie Pass turns us out; brown barrel gums, at the top.
To a sky slick and skeined in vines, to our interior
Selves. We see only what's near
                                        —lyrebirds fleeting and kerb lines.

VII
Crows in a caterwaul, honeyeater in the bottlebrush,
The day's dying symphony—strands of light in the cirrus clouds.
Everything in gravity's deep pull, the creek at its low ebb.

Peter Ramm

'Crows in a caterwaul' from Wright's *There is Balm in Gilead.*

No nursing home for hills

How my ancient body aches! My weathered slopes roll like a spool.
My skin flakes, thin and fragile; still the native grasses thrive.
Roots of kurrajong and white box burrow, trying to survive,
and goannas, quolls and tadpoles understand I'm no one's fool.

As a child I watched the tides ebb, warmed my face on lava's flow,
saw feldspar, quartz and mica crystals slowly settle out.
Oh! My teenage guts contorted; pressed and buffeted about,
then the rush of wind and water forced my granite seams to show.

I remember the first people, as a wedge-tail circles high.
I hear again their stories, as a kookaburra calls.
How they sheltered in my caves and painted pictures on the walls,
walked with wonder on my soil and fished the creeks that trickled by.

We adapted to each other, like young lovers, learned to heed.
They harvested my seeds and wove my grasses, hunted roos—
but took only what they needed, down to bark for their canoes.
As the country breathed their smoke it smiled; the wattle seeds agreed.

I remember when that new mob came and called the land their own:
built fences, yards and mansions; ploughed the earth and watched wheat
  die.
How they over-stocked the land with cloven hoofs and wondered why
so much soil washed down the creek, so many cattle shrank to bone.

Then that puffed-up squatter sold me, cold as hailstones. What a hide!
To think he thought he owned me, like a slave; no thought to share!
So the mob who'd paid the money thought they owned me, fair and square.
See, this money stuff curls human minds—they shrivel up inside.

I've lamented for an eon, now at last I grasp some hope.
Don't think my voice stays silent, for I whisper heart-to-heart.
Yes! Alert souls hear my message to plant trees and shrubs—they're smart!
They protect my soils and combat weeds; for sure, it helps me cope.

There's no nursing home for hills; I need communities to care.
My dreams depict a paradise where eucalypts grow tall:
fragrant breezes brush the tea trees, wrens and willy wagtails call,
as the people—all the people—work as one to heal. And share.

Robyn Sykes

Black wallaroo

Another dream of you, *Osphranter bernardus*,
my muscular shadow, my breathing shred

of midnight sky, perched and hunched
on the blistered lip of a splintered sandstone

grasswren scarp north of Nourlangie,
where you dream of eternal springing,

a great propulsion over sweltering, swelling
floodplains. My darkness and I are here

with you. You sense my intrusion, my confusion. You
straighten, twitch, turn, flee into a cooling

x-ray cave painted with vivid indigenous visions…
And we slip away into impenetrable gloom,

inescapable sleep, dreaming of other dawns.

Lorne Johnson

Roadkill

There is always roadkill
Bones snapped grotesque
A bloodied pelt
In a heartbeat
A Schrödinger pouch
Cars speed past
Humans with their young
Encased in polypropylene and metal
The earth now dust, dehydrated

Flora and fauna wait urgently
Rain delayed by dark satanic mills
Maybe it's not coming at all
Eucalypts move and shift
In blinding heat
Limbs graceful, thin
The spirits of ancestors
Present in the wood
The ground   the sky   the waterholes

Magpies prophesy auguries
Unreadable to invaders' eyes
The land is sentient
Its colours unique

Like an angry God,
It provides and retaliates.

We did not listen.

Viki Mealings

Menindee

Dry. Bone dry.
She exhales: hot-rust baked
from lace-wing lungs,
the dregs of the Menindee.

Bony bream:
tipped belly-ward
up-stream/down-stream
breathless in stagnant pockets,
the Darling's death pools.

Trapped, fish-bowl tight
blue-green algal oxygen suck,
jostling for the last tiny breath:
Murray Cod, among the last
to succumb.

Dry. Bone dry.
Her masters, and the primal
drive of thirst:
cotton and citrus/wheat and rice
—ballot papers.
The thirst of it, the thirst.

Irrigation.
Lakes up-stream drained again,
the take, over-allocated.
The basin fills.
The Barkindji watch on.

By bit, she muddies/slows,
blooms algal and takes on salt
—runs a temperature,
bakes (poisoned)
for 3 thousand, 2 hundred clicks,
the death litter, scooped out.

Choke-hold.
Federation hands at the last gasp
in case she gets any ideas:
jurisdictions/politicians/players
canvas the length of her body.

In Canberra, suits talk,
travel west for photo-opps,
point at things from speedboats,
wear RM Williams boots.

Dead river, dead fish
dead river, dead town
dead river, dead policy.

Which death
will matter most?

Vanessa Page

Reading the (in)land

Out back of the airbnb
you smell petrichor
on a tract of land
at the edge of the mown,
squinting at three native grasses.
You can't look them up
because there's no internet access
where you are.
The field of blue stretches
above a mottle of rain-clouds,
a dome over stock.
Branches of white cockatoos
scream across this undulating
regenerative farmland
in the Wymah Valley.

Driza-bone and Akubra,
literate in this landscape,
read *The Land.* You, however,
see this windy paddock
as bisected by metal sticks,
strands of rusty gate, wire fences,
solar array, corrugated iron water-tank.
On the coast you always
sought sea-blue skyscapes,
rock pools, wet
Sclerophyll forests.
Once inland, you don't
notice the inland ridges

tho' they've been here forever.
When you do finally pause and
take in the ragged outcrops,
your eye-balls,
more accustomed to the coast,
now follow the ancient rocky faces
and you connect to the country
for the first time.

Sally Denshire

A LENS ON BIODIVERSITY

'The bats are hanging, awake during the day.'

Amanda Anastasi

'loss suddenly
swallows me wholly
into silence.'

—All the beautiful outcasts, *Anne Casey*

'We slept in swamps to dream lichen, flowers and moss.
Came limb-to-limb with a dazzling eucalypt.'

—2035, *Angela Costi*

Speaking to the narrative

And the Minister said: 'Within
the Environmental Framework of
the here and now, we must
utilise available statistics and
forecasts to develop an alternate plan
that encompasses inherent uncertainties and
phenomena-driven adjustments to
ensure our core narrative interrogates
all available options, so
we can enhance environmental outcomes
that speak to those contestable
evaluative assessments and
articulated comments by
salient stakeholders, because
the apparent paradox within
the problematic history and
the particular inflections of
this persistent issue regarding
universal themes and
conventional patternings cannot be
ignored and thus
must be addressed within
a timeframe ...'

And the river writhed
And the trees withered
And the fish died.

Arna Radovich

This is a found poem using borrowed text from the South Australia, Murray-Darling Basin Royal Commission, *Report* (2019).

2035

Our skin grew another layer to cover the crust.
We pooled our fat to slide across the malignant terrain.

The soil fuelled our organs with microbial.
We sweated acidic waste then licked it clean.

The core heaved and vomited entrails of elder elms.
We waded inland to escape tree murder and suicide.

We slept in swamps to dream lichen, flowers and moss.
Came limb-to-limb with a dazzling eucalypt.

She was ample in girth so much like our grandmothers.
We weaved our gangrene sinews into a cradle.

When she fainted, we eased her fall to a gentle thud.
Parched bark, leafless—still a sight to behold.

Angela Costi

Drowned antechinus

Entering the writing room mid-morning I hear
the shrill, flat-line of a tree creeper, and find myself
thinking about the water skink who late last year
took up residence beneath the cabin floor
and then of a mouse my wife discovered recently
drowned in a water-bowl, the lady next door
having put out poison to protect
the eggs her chickens lay
in the coop beside the fence: the first
antechinus we've found in years
and possibly the last we will.
How long does it take
not to see something again?
A month? A decade? A life?

David Brooks

Cassowaries, Etty Bay

Cassowary Coast, Far North Qld

They stride out of prehistory.
Their gait is measured, leisurely,
a stately placing of prehensile toes
whose middle claw can kill.
There is a degree of pomp
in panoplies of plumage,
layers of black feathering
enhancing their aplomb,
a living cape from which the lofty
blue and crimson neck protrudes,
the head crowned with a casque of horn
pre-dating Babylon and Rome.

They make their regal way among
chance courtiers, the day-trippers,
posing for a photo shoot,
peering into picnic hampers,
scooping up the offerings of fruit
and choice exotic morsels,
scorning hands that reach to touch
the flounce of elegant black plumes,
slipping into rainforest like shadows
to elude the throng:

primeval apparitions that once
trod the Earth with dinosaurs
and lingered on, imprinting
after-images in sleek iPhones,
reminders of the marvellous
that vanishes as we look on,
another species that may not
survive our hegemon.

Jena Woodhouse

Lost love song

We'll never forget
songs sung in days listening
enthralled, delighted
with whispered answers near dawn
paired honeyeaters waiting

young birds ignoring
tunes for the music of love
lost to yesterday
honeyed melodies regal
rare songs now imitations

losing customed voice
once heard with morning breezes
swelling spring airwaves
with songs for mates left lonely
searching for lost lovers' tones

no chance for learning
known mating calls, enticing
young lovers' delights
calls like currawong
with cuckoo shrikes cheating love

avoiding the song
to distract wild attention,
love left too late
once long chosen melodies
are replaced with strange new calls

warbling unusual
songs taking up others' notes
false for listeners
young regent honeyeaters
craving unfulfilled by mimic

woodland overtures
from another breeding group
felled ironbark bush
leaves raucous songs, lone birds
expecting nectar and mates

learning songs again
pure bush lines memory hides
land cleared records gone
for regent honeyeaters
lost to forest destruction

Adèle Ogiér Jones

National Recovery Plan for the Regent Honeyeater (*Anthochaera phrygia*) is detailed at https://www.environment.gov.au/system/files/resources/286c0b52-815e-4a6c-9d55-8498c174a057/files/national-recovery-plan-regent-honeyeater.pdf.

All the beautiful outcasts

Stirring early to become unwitting witness
to this illicit marvel in that last gasp of intense
green (the wrong shade for the Council elite).
In between thundering freeways and sprawling
dwellings, not far from the mystery-shrouded new metro,
the unwanted tunnel that will swallow our remaining
respite of ragtag, untouched bushland—a stone's throw from
the dank shelf, a chink in the cliff where Lawson *stretched*
after sessions at the Crows Nest hotel, exchanging spontaneous
verse for a drink—is where wonder struck me post-sunrise: a flash
of flame-bright fur, a swathe of white. Undulating, sundrenched,
two entranced, entrancing fox-mates frolicking, unconscious
of anything but early warmth and each other; unmistakeable rapture
lit by the first fingers of the new day pressing between late summer's
laden branches—soaring trees classified as weeds, so easily condemned—
as easily as these magnificent, misplaced creatures. And later,
tramping past the fox bait warning signs, grief striking as
acutely as horror at the impending loss of them, and
of this vigorous corridor, alive now with spearing
lorikeets, a dive-bombing wattle-bird,
cheeks flashing red in the dead
heat where cicadas catch on, strike
up. And in all that bright, beautiful
bewitching tumult, loss suddenly
swallows me wholly
into silence. All this

flourishing
exuberance, vibrant
as those two dawn-lit outlaws;
all this precious pulsing life:
as vivid and dauntless,
as utterly unsuspecting
of their looming fate
as you had been.

Anne Casey

The italicised words are taken from a heritage sign posted adjacent to Henry Lawson Cave in Flat Rock Gully Reserve, Sydney, which commemorates one of Australia's best-loved bush poets.

One hundred flashing corellas

just flew over, squawking the sky into shimmering
fragments of wavering v-lines, puffed with billowing
cumulus, awkward as misplaced apostrophes.

It stings imagination. On another day this same summer sky
was filled with crying, lost and hungry, madly-flapping
forest red-tailed black cockatoos, haunted by ceaseless
destruction of banksia woodland which used to stretch forever,
filled with endemic nuts to crack and swallow. These lost souls
prey now on berries from foreign trees filled with distance
and otherness—their wandering tuned to wondering.

Far away from native fields of sustaining flora
long since bulldozed to sand and anger—
some small parts left as roadside remnants and in
a few acres reserved for just in case—
corellas swing low and noisesome over swaying fields
of wheat, green-gold husks holding swelling embryos of grain
and longing. Puzzled white cockies muster in their thousands,
monopolising like storm clouds that vastness of broken sky
and unspoken, crippling displacement.

I look for answers in fallen feathers,
like counting rings in a clear-felled karri
to reveal the pain and stain of why,
but there are none to find. A lot
of people have a lot to answer for.

Allan Padgett

commune-banded

Urtica incisia family *Urthicacene.* Stinging Nettle.

Nut-brown, black-currented, honeyed, buttered, muddied stutter the tribes of flowers. Flourished-hatted some, oblivious, knowingly protected on the host, not to be victimised. Cluster cloistered and tugged, pulled in close; not crumpled but crowded, not unsettled, but if standing out then elegant, celebratory, thinking outwards. Or standing gathered outside an iron-aged-peopled kingdom.

Dark-Christmas-tree green-leaved narrowed top to broadened bottom. Pike-ramparted. Spiked-haired to annoy/make cross, hairs speared, sworded, readied at their launching pad. Hairs everywhere.

A clan-commune community-banded, mustering in full force of battalions.

Moya Costello

Inter-wishing

I'm more impressed by
                    a tangled embracing biodiversity
                              a homeostasis of home harmonised
not by a diamond shower
      on Jupiter
      in millions
or by the singularity of water on
                  both
sides
    of the moon

our virtual imaginings of these takings
accept a diminutive nature of our terrenity
extinguish all my earth-bound experiences
make my whole life of no benefit to any life

yet ascending with the old regular moon is
an eternal faithfulness to the tides of our lives
a summons to synchronous coral spawning
a compass for a zillion lives in the darkness

and my inter-wishing
               for Earth
for every generation of every organism
to clasp us into a breathless sensation
of phosphorescence and foliaceousness
to remain immersed in a terraqueous life.

Caterina Mastroianni

On a day

that saw everyone as childlike
or as someone with whom to identify

the day, not this day
was one for striped bandicoots

or dwarf bettongs that are an unlikely
combination of rat and kangaroo

the day recognised this as elliptical
or enigmatic and spoke to everyone

individually, as if another species
it said, *if you take away one*

you detract from another
in a muted language of air

Ann Shenfield

Failing to see regent honeyeaters at Springfield Lakes

The photons were aging; it was the dying light we parked under;
a goliath eucalypt shielded us from the sun's spray, like some
cliff face—moss bearded, will splinter a waterfall's spring melt.
Or braiding platinum hair into twin spikes, a white-moustached
stockman bending to drink from an ancient soak. There was
a splitting of substance, some insight we gained momentarily,
but at a terrible cost. A light & darkness war raged throughout
Springfield Lakes; it was that time of the day; magic hour, where
dulled light turned the pond's surface black as wrought iron.
Where we needed to put our backs to the sun's rays, shield eyes
from residual glare, like trying to hide from an atomic blast
behind a trunk's thick factory wall. I sat in the rear, a banished
child trying to work out exactly where the honeyeaters had been
seen at this artificial well, only twenty minutes from home.
An antithesis of the sixth extinction event, some strange reversal
of feathered fortune. Or a heart that rallies right at the end.
They shouldn't have been here at all. In this blighted oasis.
They shouldn't have landed right next to the café, waiter polite,
serving up an ignorant delicacy for their customers. Right
in a sandpaper fig's folded grey napkin as they dug for sugary lerp.
In the goldilocks zone of the expresso machine's warning hiss.
This was all too slanted, as the light cut like wind into our eyes.
This wasn't ironbark woodland, but renovated park with polished
boardwalks, kids' swings, joggers lapping the lake, exercising their
knowledge of real estate. The distant murmuring was the M2,
not some nearby creek. & beyond that a commuter train's brakes
vented to a stop like a V1 dropping onto a city. We speculated.
Impossible migrants. Refugees from some southern fire disaster.
A magnetic compass malfunction in their brain's walnut kernel.

Even a remnant population that had somehow escaped the slaughter
of their nesting sites in South-East Queensland. There was no reason
why the black & olive honeyeaters, locally extinct, had flown straight
into noisy miner heartland of broken suburban bush, where
developers overlayed their sandstone walls on this ironbark refuge
—the UN trying to pacify some ravaged border, with a DMZ.
Exiting the car, their territorial calls chipped away at ice with an axe.

The ironic hobby: birdwatching with my daughter; the monstrous
hate she has for the sun that pushes her in the back of the eyes.
Her detest for open spaces, for anywhere new that her memory
hasn't mapped out as safe. Glare-caught as a marsupial grazing
in the cool night air, she operated under the cover of Sydney blue
gums, their black capes donning her shoulders, their ripe nectar
clogging her nostrils like a chloroformed handkerchief.
The regent honeyeaters' jizz meaningless as the phantom limbs
of false rails & stairs that crowd out her territory. After a fruitless
fifteen minutes we called it quits, as miners filleted the pale-yellow
eucalypt flowers with their slaughterhouse beaks; dumb to their
eternal role pollinating our drowning world. Even if they were there,
right in front of us in the draining coffee-ground darkness, the regent
honeyeaters just donned their ghillie suits & disappeared

BR Dionysius

Dream beaches, Safety Bay

All is translucent turquoise and serene.
Beyond the rippled mirror of the water's fractured edge
Where castles washed away by last night's tide
Every sunny singing day on the golden snoozing sands
We wait together for epiphany.
Drifting in the grottoes where shy sharks
Slither out of sight
Deaf to the playful surfbreaks on the distant roaring reef
We dance with clownfish, play with starfish
The paintful blue of damsels and dancing angels
Striped in black and white
Score the scuba choreography for our delight.
Beyond the hazy dunes the noon sun
Bakes the vast dry heart
On ancient shores where shells and bones
Are turned to stone.

The robot dinosaurs dig old red country's wounds
To launch these fragments of a sacred heart
From violated beaches
To poisoned continents that float on desecrated seas
Where there are no dreamers bedded safely on the shore.
No sea is wide or wild enough to spare
The dreamers on the beach
From waking in the brilliant light
of the last morning of the surf.

Silver bright as flickering jewels
the countless fishes wait their turn
As one by one the hunters swallow them
to disappear forever—like a dream.

Annie Hill Otness

snails/rain

they practice their revolution
gingerly. The cool is a giant
shell, glistening as condominium
fences lather in mucus. Droplets
remaining droplets, they are—now
free of salt/ pesticides—intent
as continental drift; concrete walls
glitter with their slipstreams/ship wakes
 n waves—They
inch to their moist polling stations
endlessly, pooling and semi-seen but
easy to ignore on tarmac, returning
no light, you observe. The burning/stars.

Josie/Jocelyn Deane

Feral cat

for Badger

You look like you belong
in a garden, serenely soft,
nested on flagstones
puddled in sun,
safe between the fences.

Bloodied chin and paws
ripe with feathers,
you swallow
the smallest victims
in slow, insolent bites.

After all, this is your role:
to forage, take vermin,
dodge the boot. One of the lesser
beasts, doing a job that suits.
Cat carves a name.

This time and place
was not your choice,
but you have always been expert
at making do with humans.
But you, kitten, are not feral.

You were born in the dark,
wet and slick amongst the hay.
Your mother, avid hunter,
died of tiger bite. I took you
home, nursed on powdered milk.

Your curved pads track,
hunt birds through screens.
Now, thirteen years on,
I syringe pap twice a day
to keep you alive.

All needles and pills,
your exhausted belly
cannot move,
but you still have this—
the sun and wind.

You have lived longer
than nature intended.
Your brethren strip feathers,
raid nest, swallow whole lines.
I know you would do the same—

after all, this is a partnership
of equals
on the most destructive scale.
I trace a brilliance in your eyes,
haunting and bright and cold as mirror.

Siobhan Hodge

reverse osmosis

we inhale mineral rivers
through interwoven roots
oxygen ions lift our ribs
expand our inner trees

between bronchial branches
our godlike mirror image
blossoms narcissistic
clots in saline pools

we share acidic airs
recycle pleural lies
a xylem of contagion
closes our phloem throats

plantation tissues ooze
chlorophyll corpuscles
coagulate our plasma
stem interstitial seas

carbons race our pulses
circulate visceral ash
combust viral receptors
wheeze our divine name

we ringbark our own trunks
haemorrhage syrup tar
harvest lethal excess
hoard cold alveoli fruit

forests around our hearts
reweave us in cilia roots
reabsorb our reflection
exhale us in mineral rivers

Nicole Rain Sellers

Spectacled flying-foxes

Pteropus conspicillatus

Unfurling into evening, grotesque
black blooms that drink the dark,
they metamorphose into screeching
raiders on a spree, ascending
from the dense dome of the century-
old fig tree, inscribing fading sky
with living, wavering calligraphy.

Attuned to the nychthemeral
that siphons energy from night,
they are released by waning light
to soar into deep indigo—
cryptic glyphs dispersing into dusk
before the ink has dried,
serrated wings untiring
in their foraging trajectories.

Night vision can detect the palest
blossom; a keen sense of smell
makes them connoisseurs of the delectable:
nectars whose intoxicating scents
intensify at twilight;
fruits exuding esters so that taste-buds
effloresce. Flying-foxes sip white flowers,
rip open soft mango skins to feast
on the ambrosia of golden flesh.

Converging and descending cohorts,
homeward bound as darkness thins,
cluster in the dim and leafy corridors
of native fig. Drawing in wing-segments
to resemble furled umbrellas,
elders mount a guard at the periphery
while others roost—wrapped in leather capes
on bleaker days; unfurling them in heat,
displacing air with languid strokes
to raise a breath of breeze;
swaddling the newborn in maternal
wings until night falls, when infants
ride out on the quest for nectar,
clamped to mothers' teats.

Looping earth to firmament,
mammals that can fly—
unique beings whose fig tree seems
a home in perpetuity
pass the days agreeably,
in naps and grooming, sunbathing,
chattering with neighbours in an amicable way.

Jena Woodhouse

The century-old fig tree outside the Cairns central library housed a thriving colony of critically endangered Spectacled flying-foxes, which was forcibly relocated (i.e. evicted) in 2020, even as females were giving birth. Declared endangered in February 2019, they already qualified as critically endangered, according to official guidelines. Source: Australian Wildlife Protection Council website: https://awpc.org.au/http:/awpc.org.au/topics/uncategorized/state-by-state/queensland/ Accessed 15 February 2021.

Dance of the river gums

The broad sweep of a sleepy riverbed emerges, timidly, from its shroud of darkness. A child seeking to scale either bank would soon find the need to proceed on all fours; hunched, nose to the ground, reminiscent of an echidna sniffing out a meal. Formed into a close-knit garrison, a dozen reeds stand to attention, to the left of centre, where the ground is still boggy from the remains of recent rain. On the right, a few shallow pools tremble at the touch of morning air. At last, some early light, and the performers begin; each one looping ribbons of bark behind their back like a stately gentleman whose braces have slipped from his shoulders to fall where they please. Amid the uncertainty of dawn, a new dancer steps forward, only to step back; the way young people fall in and out of love. The scene fills with daylight, river gums bounce and sparkle, leaves dangle at the oddest of angles, reflections from the pools lift the leading members of the troupe before gently setting them down once more. Imperceptibly, the sun heads higher until the day is undeniable and each artist assumes their most statuesque pose. At which point, a wallaby twitches the last of the dew from his whiskers, a tawny frogmouth pretends not to notice and a couple of diamond sparrows make their way, unhurriedly, in and out of the shadows; the way old people fall in and out of love, and back in again.

Gregory Piko

Revelation

When I am dust
mere rumour discussed among leaves
who will guard my trees?

Will swaying limbs
be felled, harvested for intransient wealth
or left to rot—an inconvenience to development?

Will the sky erupt
hurl cartwheels of flame, ignite standing trees
black matchsticks ablaze?

Or steeped in waste
will they bulge, mutate, form violated shapes,
or simply wither?

Still, I *will* plant seedlings,
some things warrant hope, some things permit
trust,

like fingers raised or wise message sticks
they may well live to tell of biodiversity, these
my scattered trees.

Joy Reid

Survival

She's back again this year
in heels and nuptial plumes,
coquettish
in pale eye liner
            —the white-faced heron
selecting twigs,
thinking of survival

What rush of rapture
bursts
            —these birds
designed from
templates of dinosaurs
with songs that shiver
in the deep wells of the soul

So, despite
the cracking ice
in Greenland, the rift,
the cleft, the split,
the speld

Despite the smell,
the stench, the stink
of burning forest,
I see you still,

framed
by cross-thatched leaves,
your changing of the guard
with stilt-stepped stealth,
this private pact
between you,
this brooding hope
—triumphant

John Bartlett

2049

You don't remember bees. I draw one for you,
filigree the wings in silver. Snow is something

the freezer does when you don't close the door
properly. Blue skies are daily and the moon's

lost its face. Sea levels have risen, no more
treks to the tide collecting shells. You giggle

at photos of me in tights and long sleeves.
Gloves are displayed in museums like aliens.

Ice cream shares have shot through the roof,
you ask me how many flavours I can name.

Another skin treatment's launched to make
it harder to burn (I'll never confess my sunbed

hours). Swimming is law, treading water the new
gym. You joke your kids will have webbed feet.

JV Birch

Eco

I've lost my tail
the claws are bitten-down stubs
          wings have shrivelled from neglect
                    those hollow bones are moans.

It may be spring but the leaves are still falling.
A rain-spit hits soil, there's no permeation…
runoff scribbles obituary all down towards the city drains.

Even fire has lost interest as it roots about
the debris that once called itself forest floor.
Feathers hide in soot. Fur sits in dismal clumps
& this is no seasonal moult.

I am of no use,
woodchips are fashionable this year.
If they scrape the lot
there may be soybean crops for a year or so.

Les Wicks

The Australian Anthropo-seen

Up there
in the gumtree, we see the unmistakable
symbol of the Australian bush—the humble koala
(*Phascolarctos cinereus*). Those large round fluffy ears
make it easy to hear what is happening up high
& down low. Hazelnut eyes watch
while a large spoon-shaped nose
remains ready to determine the levels
of toxic molecules in any given eucalyptus
leaf. The humble koala's wholly dependent
on eucalypt forests: its sole source of sustenance
and shelter. This arboreal marsupial is adaptable yet vulnerable to the effects
of global warming. The ever-increasing CO_2 levels in Earth's atmosphere
have begun to change the chemical composition of
eucalyptus leaves, raising concentrations of tannins
& reducing concentrations of proteins to the point
where nutritional value is compromised. Meanwhile, the flames
of Australia's increasingly intense bushfire seasons burn more
& more koalas & their gumtree homes.
These changes may be more than our
symbolic marsupial
can stand.

Michael J Leach

Birders

Instead of smelting steel or driving
forklifts at the port, men are buying bird
books, spotting, making blogs, competing.
Last week, Pete scored a willow warbler.
Harry beat that with an orange-breasted
whinchat. Wildlife centres springing
up where smokestacks once belched
hot air and muck. Dads and granddads
walking lads out over marsh,
telling tales of birds' long journeys.
Places where they fed, watered,
rested in sanctuaries now disappeared.

In the hide, men whisper names—
shoveler, pochard, lapwing,
redshank—once a glossy ibis.
The lads are their apprentices.
Men help to adjust the lenses
of binoculars, so that when
they close one eye and squint,
they see
the world changed
            for birds and men.

Moya Pacey

The visitor from Bahrain

Dawn blew a bright gold bubble hued
with mother-of-pearl and drew a road
through the middle, with paddocks and
trees on either side, and kangaroos
all focused on one question—was that
a killer going down to the creek?

He stops in his gravel-grinding steps and
raucous in the silence hears his thoughts,
squawking on regardless. The kangaroos
have stunned him—their singular eyes
pinned upon him, their anachronism—
he reaches for his camera-cum-phone.

But the mob is taking no chances. His stick
drops to the ground. They spring into motion,
a brown wave beating across the earth's
weed-encrusted brow. Nothing in his
hemisphere of pacing, prowling, pack-
laden animals has prepared him for this.

For the power in their curved tails, each
effortless arc releasing, then returning
to gather momentum. He has triggered
a maelstrom, feels the whole tableau was
engineered for him; senses rainbow skins
of memory, enveloping time and space.

The trees here seem to fall upon their feet,
he thinks, noting the glint on their sickle-bladed
leaves. He breathes their breath, their generous
hospitality, recalls the lonely tree of life. Down
to the half-moon water he hurries, hoping
a platypus might surface, swimming strongly.

Matina Doumos

fine

Lachnagrostis filiformis (G. Forst.) Trin. family *Poaceae*. Blown Grass/Fairy Grass.

fine fine fishing line thin
pale palea lime-green mellow-yellow straw-feathered
feathered-sheathed
fishing-line fine minutely membranous
spiked-seeded
blade striped shallowly grooved
blown (wind) grass hairy (woolly) grass thread-shaped
pattern-embroidered
fine fine entanglement panicle spreading divaricated
abscission in windblow
independently assertively not shy caring-for

Moya Costello

Bowerbird blues

Dear Human,
Where's all the blue plastic?
My lady friend found it fantastic.
She'd visit my bower
for hour upon hour.
The absence of plastic is drastic.

The clothes pegs were popular treasure.
I'd plot and I'd plan and I'd measure
just where to place them.
Intruders, I'd chase them.
My lady could browse at her leisure.

Bottle caps added some fun,
randomly placed one by one.
My style was eclectic.
My work pace was hectic.
She'd visit to see what I'd done.

Now I'm foraging hour after hour
for a beautiful feather or flower.
I'm terribly tired
but my lady's inspired.
She's agreed to remain at my bower.

Pat Simmons

Waitaramoa Creek haiku

1

Dragonfly hovers
above the weed-rotting creek
methane bubbles rise.

2

Kowhai petals float
bright yellow on smoky black
slowly drifting round.

3

A shortage of rain
causes the algae to bloom
a viscous yellow.

4

Forty days of drought
and desperate wasps patrol
the last two puddles.

Piers Davies

DÉGUSTATION

AMUSE BOUCHE

Tender shark bite w/ cured wagyu sliver
& polypropylene relish on crisp
rhinoceros horn rosti

APÉRITIF

Spearmint algae bloom guilt gyre

HORS D'OEUVRE

Warm sourdough w/ hard-boiled hummingbird
eggs, shredded vulture belly, blood
diamonds & seedless wild rose jam

ENTRÉE

Carbon sink beluga bisque w/ arctic krill,
kauri fungi, smoked orangutan
emulsion & gold leaf

REMISE EN BOUCHE

Bittersweet cumquat chlorine sorbet

PLAT PRINCIPAL
Flaming humanity skewers in a
benzodiazepine demi-glace w/ wilted jungle
microgreens, sundried seahorses, sleet
vinaigrette & rock art dust

DESSERT
Deconstructed quicksand trifle w/
drunken box jellyfish medusa, shattered
honeycomb & whitewash crème froth

DIGESTIF
Decadent particulate-percolated
nightshade toddy

Nicole Rain Sellers

Salvage

Show us the frontier, devil ray
giant divergent from sharks; Jurassic
whip-tail evolved out the sting;
gentle bat-like fish that wings
itself each side of sea play;
secret-keeper for fossil-rare
and death-by-captivity—
so little we know
beside the mask you show.

Inspired, hull-mired
at the flotsam-line,
filter feeder becomes sea cleaner:
steel cephalic fins guide rubbish in,
cycles plastic to synthetic gas
through turbines into power
so self-sustained, late Anthropocene
tech-adept manta-totem boat
repurposes; redeems.

When trash streams clear
adaptations will make
brown murk disappear.
Retool, morph again for
kelp farms, forests
to machine a future where
old treasures unlock: oxygen,
clean water and underseas teemed
with streams of baby manta rays.

Rebecca Trowbridge

Silky oak

Grevilliea robusta

Trophy parts.
The dismembered:
thud-echoes to
          amber litter to
                    vanished
bright, curved hands, tumbling bright
cleaved loose from timber:
limb
by limb
                    milled,
framing up the south-east corner
and beyond.

Rosenstengel's pin-up
each torso measured twice,
sawn and fashioned into function:
weighing down
          the curled-up corners
          of hot-box bedrooms
clinging steadfast
to dwellings of timber and tin
window joinery and panels.

Grevillea robusta
her resilience, a force
          across drought seasons:
          holding fast
                    to loam and basalt
decades before legislators

slowed axes
growing quietly,
          bearing relaxed thicknesses
                    of honey coils,
ready for bees.

Beyond a firebreak,
                              appraised
by new craftsmen
oceans distant
in *Larrivee*'s workshops
the length of her body
worked carefully
          to fine, fluid
                    acoustic shells:
                              strummed.

Vanessa Page

Brixton Street Wetlands

The lopped heads of tuarts bare red-ringed eyes
towards the heavens. Growing loops cut back,
the cockatoos scream overhead. Theirs is a horror
for the homeless. Head of family bent under tyre
tread that troops through swamp. The acrid smoke
over fermented leaves and the relief
of peppermint gums. Heads of state pray
jobs, jobs, jobs
the same old song, the same old state
of play. What we need most. Crystal Brook
closed for business. Priority species slip
beneath another portfolio, all on desks
and office suites far from the killing field.
Dead tuarts stretch for the sun. Appropriate controls
look so much better on paper.

Siobhan Hodge

Recurrences

Underneath the canopy I have my hands in the comfort of soil,
exploring around your roots, I dream of a bulb's spring flowering.
Yellow bells, ephemeral at the foot of an elegant bark brown column.
Your tree's life eclipses mine, but we are both gentle beings
snarled in Earth's current ferment, weathering threats together.

Storms bring lightening, firing up the very spine and trunk of us,
burning into heart's wood, cracking limbs and my resolve.
Then drought sucks at the ground, baring our mother's bones,
until inevitably floods return, and inundated by despair,
I begin to fall apart. But you endure.

You, who cannot walk away,
speak to me in creaking whispers
with your voice of chlorophyll and lignin.
Saying that this is only our planet's long staccato song.
Sometimes the winds play fair, sometimes changes blow us over,
that's all.

In the comfort of soil I find a snail shell's circular recurrences
and here among the debris of the storm, a bulb's blunt finger
pushes through.

Elspeth Findlay

A LIKELY HABITAT

'The wildflowers think it is Spring.'

Amanda Anastasi

'We are
the land, and we undo our very selves.
It is time / to heal, my loves, so we don't lose it all.'

—Tidewrack, *John Robert Grogan*

'through the stubble
of last season's oats, a following of swallows picks
disturbed insects from yellowing grass. Welcome
swallows....'

—When an owl dies, *Sandra Renew*

Breathing above the benthos

breathing above the benthos beneath me
capillary waves encircle my breath like strands of floating hair
solace snorkels across fragmented pauses of metamorphosis

breathing above the benthos beneath me
I colour in flowerpots, cauliflowers, fingers, organs
swim for deeper reefs fished out by terrestrial eyes

breathing above the benthos beneath me
white-water waves surge and spill shocking screw-ups, crashing
onto my murmuring mermerosity until it amplifies in unison

breathing above the benthos beneath me
in this seabed of uneasy truths and transformations
I surrender to the biomimicry that creates breath.

Caterina Mastroianni

Mermerosity: An anticipatory state of being worried about the possible passing of the familiar and its replacement by that which does not sit comfortably in one's sense of place.
—Earth Emotions: *New Words for a New World*, Glenn A. Albrecht

Catch water. Hold fire.

A small yellow bird vacates its tree to nest in the antlers of a stag.

On this first of seven days away, a woman and man are out walking.
They pass a dying riverbed, evidence of a larger system in mourning.

A thin scrim of wind agitates the ranger's warning they should
anticipate rain. They come to a clearing, scoop dirt, gather wood.

She selects stones to edge the hollow fonts he fashions in the dry,
unyielding earth; one will catch water, the other hold fire. At dusk,

they prepare a meal they devour with raw, percussive pleasure.
Afterwards, they lie down beside the fire. Neither of them speaks.

When they sleep their fingers touch. Blood-lightning courses back
and forth between them. The man dreams of slow-flowing lava,

of times she'd cry out when they made love, as when she'd first heard
the humpbacks singing. The woman dreams beside him. Manta rays

skim her seas in impossibly tight formations. On their second morning,
they give thanks for bark-softening mist—no rain—and for their seven days

away. They gorge on books and berries on their third day. When darkness
comes, they drop like falling pinecones in front of the fire.

On the fourth day they hunt for stray songs and on the fifth, write a list
of things they might one day require for storytelling. Or survival.

Her eyes are white-hot embers on the sixth day when she offers to recite
the Periodic Table of Elements, elaborating for him the fugitive
properties

of Tellurium. There are three things, he says on the seventh day, that love
requires proximity for—to eat together, walk together, bed together.

The word he uses is aggregate. Love aggregates, he says, in blood,
muscle, skin and bone. The man and woman lean into a kanuka tree.

The small yellow bird listens from its nest in the stag's antlers.

Claire Beynon

Twin pines

Away for the weekend only
but when we get home—most
likely to improve the view
from the new houses on Laetitia Street—
someone's cut down the two giant pines
the white cockatoos have been
roosting in as long as we can remember.

Instead of the twilight's raucous tattoo
as they settle for the night
there's now a desolate emptiness, one
hundred and twenty nests
chipped with the rest,
eggs, chicks, fledglings, and all
the survivors flown.

No more white carnage in the paddock
as they root for the native corms, no more
gathering to drink from the spill-trough, no more
stomping about
at first light on the veranda roof, their
absence fills the valley,
a tense, directionless plea.

David Brooks

The flood

The civility of seasonality is all washed up.
Now it dumps on everyone, careless as climate change.
We'll take the fall; it's all sheeted down to us.

An elemental forced its way into my room one night.
First the windows imploded, then the walls caved.
It picked up everything, churning, turning it all over, ballistic.

It found me hunched and punched the little water bag of my body
into its solution, made me flotsam like the rest of my rubbish.
Made me understand the nature of oblivion.

Elspeth Findlay

We of the Merri Merri are not a pathetic fallacy

You call us River Gums. We don't mind. We are all family, even though your botanists call us different names—Swamp Gum, Red Box, Red Stringybark, Manna Gum, Grey Box, Yellow Box. Even the She-oaks don't mind your botanists' names. After all, those names are pretty literal. We hope they remind you we just are. Listen: we sway and creak in the wind. This doesn't mean we don't feel, hear, see. We do. We see further than you. Today the story begins with a human jogging along the Merri Creek (we don't give you names, assign you a species, genus or gender). They're oblivious to the whipping of their pony tail on their cheekbones. Oblivious to the amber baubles of bitter Kangaroo apples they stomp past step after step as they loop their way back under the bridge. They're thinking about gyrfalcons. How they fly out and always return, even when the leash breaks. We snicker at the fantasy. But we shouldn't. The Eutaxia and Honey Pots shiver. Huddle and droop from sight. We sway and creak. Know better than to say aloud their pony tail drags them back to the nearby bushes. We smell leather, the pale hood falling over her eyes. Yes, we know they are a young woman (it's an old story). We saw her assailant. He took her through her skin thin bark. A sound like the cry of the tawny frogmouth in the thick of night. But it is dusk, and already the haunting begins. A helicopter hovers over the wetlands. Our whispers are cut to the quick. We flap our ears shut. You will hear the whirring and buzzing and droning all through the night. You will toss and turn, imagining the young woman's whereabouts. You already know that the psychologist will fail to take action. You know that the only witness will refuse to testify.

The rapist will get off lightly. It's an old story. Next morning, you'll not listen to the news. You'll get up and dress in the dark. Then you will lace up your running shoes. And run. Don't plug your ears. Watch out for us. We see what you can't see. We record what you call the invisible. Our fibres are feelers growing thick with rumours.

Dominique Hecq

With words like doom-scrolling…

what century are we in? What time is it?

From across the closed world you tell me
you imagine your bookshelf as a row of edible leaves.

I order my days as a Vermeer woman in an apron—
baking bread, taking time to make the bed, the one I lie on

drowning in white noise I call the Hum.
The other day, I don't know which one, I heard a call.

It was new to my garden.
I wanted to understand how Time had lodged itself

in that black-capped turn
of a curious head. It had one eye cocked

giving me the time of day
before setting off on some miraculous migration.

Or was it, like me, here to stay?

In some loose part of me I hoped it would never end—
this day, this reckoning sky

now open to conversations with small things
climbing stairs an hour each day

my solo trek to the top of the mountain
enough oxygen to make my way down

Julie Maclean

Provider

'Breathe,' you whisper
in a silent shimmy of delight
at the connection I have found
between socks and tyres, coffee
and shelter to beetles—
the gifts you have given while dead,
and alive, a place for tracing shadows
with light, as even now,

in contemplation, my sweat decays
your fibrous cover, I cup your spine
of hardened glue, bled by others
to your binding as I pick you apart
leaf by leaf, how you talk,
how you come to me, from South,
my library—this lovely tome,
The Wisdom of Trees

Trees,
The wisdom of this lovely tome
from my library, South,
how you come to me,
how you talk as I pick you apart,
leaf by leaf to your binding,
of hardened glue, bled by others,
I cup your spine, your fibrous cover
my sweat decays in contemplation,

as, even now, with light
a place for tracing shadows
while alive, while dead,
the gifts you have given:
shelter for beetles,
coffee, tyres and socks, I have found
the connection in a shimmy of delight,
you whisper
'Breathe.'

Gail Ingram

Setting the rain free

She carefully hands me the rain in a basement
carpark in the belly of this concrete city.
I hide it in an ordinary looking bag,
sleight of hand so no one recognises these
molecules gathered to turn love opaque.

I cover the rain in blankets,
muffling gentle drumming
to no more than a hypnotic beat.

I drive steadily so as not to create suspicion.
The border guards are lazy,
will not give me a second thought.

I push deep into the country, wait until it's dark
—cold starlit sky, a thousand beams of time gone by—
remove the blankets, unzip the bag
with these driftwood fingers,

set the rain free so powdered pearls
will sing again to the sea,
translucent threads swirl joyful,
capture of dust,
red drops roll
rusty to the forest floor.

Create new skies to drown us once again,
our tears heaven faced
as we flee this broken Ark.

Geoff Callard

Turnings

Season of mystic metamorphoses,
of shifted sets, old shapes expunged,
switched-colour outfits rearranged,
when there's no turncoat more bizarre than these:

a crowd of mutant crested cockatoos,
their bodies thinned to slender stalks,
their clownish heads like gaudy jokes,
faces all flushed, with startled green hairdos.

Give them a second glance, and they'll appear
in quite another guise: dressed so
like florid marsupial mitts—presto!
Let's think of it as Ovid's time of year,

when this converts to that, and that in turn
to something else.... But how it'll all
turn out—ah, there's a different tale!
Climate awry? Then must our emperor spurn

the poet of transformations, turn him out
of home into a cold exile?
No further spring beyond the pale?
Last post for Ceres? Not a seed of doubt?

Or can the quick-change artist yet improve
our lot by cultivating tropes
to freshen an empire's faded hopes
of turning a corner—so we all survive?

Ian Reid

Noise coils the hollow

Noise coils the hollow
hum of empty train carts
no coal that direction.

On the other track
every full carriage
carries a part
of this land's belly.

The womb of the valley left barren
the glowing horizon lit humanly
an amphitheatre of loss
like bony hips
hollow.

My house is full of ghosts
other lands cry into rooms
fill the spaces with their distance.
I adorn my body with remnants
of another land's heart.

A piece of South Africa on my windowsill,
quartz from Cape Town
a friend had carried
all the way back.

Thai orchid petals
hang crisp in resin from gold chain
and my greenstone Toki pendant
has the hush of the long white cloud.

Ancient trees made my daybed
a forest far from here left weeping
and I rest.

My Ghanaian warrior,
the carved wooden woman,
holds a candle to her shape-shift
waxing the story of her past.

And the steel shrieks under train-trawler
sheeting its sad cry across night.
At the coast
coal loader waits with hungry ships.

There goes another belly of a mountain
across oceans
always away.

Open wounds

heavy air
the ghost of what's lost.

Gillian Swain

I am not doing anything

And when my heart for all this ending
shrinks to the size of a frozen pea,
and when I want to close the blinds,
Netflix and chill until I forget there is any ocean,
let alone this one, charging forth to eat us all,
—too trite to say it serves us right—
I make myself recall the birds, fallen,
the bandicoots and desert rats, the frogs I
wish I had kissed into princes before they left
what now remains of Earth.
Bats. Koalas. Rivers of fish. I make my mind bring up
beaches: shore erosion felling homes, forests: now ash and dust,
sky: daily smoke haze. I could list extinctions and endangerments
until our eyes burst with the build-up of unshed tears,
but this way lies madness, medication
and more endless TV of forgetting.
Episode after episode. When I can no longer turn
the Anthropocene into a HD essay,
recite readily consumed lists of deaths,
I spend my time reading up on the burden of overwhelm—
this is as useless as everything else.

Ivy Ireland

An immortal contemplates her plastic heart

Why did I laugh tonight?—John Keats

our close cousins the homo sapiens
believed the heart held our souls
held our earliest memories
held our truest heart of hearts
cells of the heart are steadfast
from the tube to the grave
but all that has changed

today universal reality crafted
extinct stratocumulus clouds—
they are everyone's favourite
all day my sisters threw about
Latin names for myriad lost birds
elucidating delicate feathers
but why bother, they fly away

heart, you and I are here
or you are not here, am I here?
heart, you are a clenched fist
holding a garish bucket of rust-
red wine that only I can drink,
to be so privileged is a sacrifice—
blood pours down my chin

in one and the same subject
two opposing motions—gushing
and pumping—repentance
and desire—I am dragged
with my heart-shaped seed
down into sub-zero darkness
of new doomsday chamber

mother, you cannot save me—
I no longer remember you,
you died before my first rebirth,
crocus corm sown upside-down
with untethered bearings, I grew
inward—my sorrows and triumphs
erased in a way I hardly noticed

I'm just a little tired I guess,
single x'ers are the hardest
to bear—they used to be men,
my heart, we are dispossessed
from time, and serious matters
pertaining to your kind, but we
are here, you and I, for a while

Jennifer Allen

His volts light me up when I wake

'the future, for which I really worked, is mine'—Nikola Tesla

I'm high in my eyrie looking down
on claret ash turned blood   not a cloud interrupting
and only yesterday
lightning strikes
from his experimental towers
reached all the way here

Venus was stopped in her oddball orbit
by his starched bow tie   ironed spotless
and I remembered what you said
so I looked for his grief and found the injured pigeon
nursed back to life and loved, he said
like a woman   like a Serbian poem

There are times I flicker
with ten books open   empty bottle and a change of season
creeping over my trees in the form of a sky with a bad attitude
and that stillness in the air

And he's here   my Hallelujah hero!
stepping out of his invisibility cloak
screwing enough sun in a single battery
to my white white wall
threatening to shake every atom
in every blackening cell
every shiver
of my darker than dark   dark matter

Julie Maclean

The intransigence of clouds

When the great currents turn away and clouds refuse to fall pregnant,
we look at their flat bellies with the sad wistfulness of childless parents
standing in blackened dust, our tears too salty to quicken seed to green.

The land seems absent from itself. It has gone underground into its heart
leaving stony ribs of range and fire dried plains to whisper songs of
past millennia,
remembering other bony times, when trees died, sighing sideways
into desert.

Inland, turbines have quit their wining, pipes are hollow highways
for animals.
Windmills sag, dams retreat to brackish brown, turning empty eyes to space.
It is a grave time. In the mud they're making fossil records for the
future to find.

We have turned our backs on all that. Talk of climate change is
un-Australian.
From inside shoreline high rises, we observe the surf, sparkling with
plastic detritus.
Oceans of last resort are fouled but, refined many times, the Pacific
is potable.

Ceilings make fine skies, environments reside inside, conditioned air
is best,
pale bodies are beautiful. Rain like sweet champagne, will only make
you sick.
Ersatz is the new nature. We don't need the damned intransigence of clouds.

Elspeth Findlay

Keep the wheels turning

Queue three deep
Tin cars gasping for liquid
Traffic lights blinking
Engine hot with fury
Over a barrel at cost of a litre

Nudge forward
Within reach of umbilical cord
Pulsing with life
Rich blood
Pumping through veins

Close the mouth
When the belly is full
Nothing but dirt around lips
Remnants leaving putrid
Smell on hands

Swipe the plastic
Conversation in any language
Lining deep pockets
In the commodity rich countries
Sitting on a well

Turn the ignition key
Satisfied purr into action
Nose out into traffic
Hit open road
Burn rubber on black tarmac

Groundhog Day
Top up when gauge is down
Bank account empty
Money burns
Faster than fuel

Need gas to move
From here to there
To keep turning hot wheels
Of my vocal cords
Crying out for help

Kelly Van Nelson

Civilisations

At 3 am local time
they dim the cabin lights
the tube becomes a womb
of soft colours ebbing from the edges.

Far below, without us realising
they fight a continuing war
for their freedom; a war many
will never live to see the end.

An hour later we pass over
slums, shacks built from splinters
beggars without eyes
children dying from a disease
that could be cured by a single pill.

While arms and ammunitions are shipped
secretly to embargoed sects
into the hands of those dying children
who point and shoot as if playing
with plastic poisonous pistols.

But we will never know about that.
We will wake at 6 am for another
breakfast. The lights will show
us all the way to our blind spots.

Lincoln Jaques

Tidewrack

It is time to heal, my loves. Time for us
to be a sea of change. Look, the chips are
down and there is no more time to fight. I
wish I could keep my mouth shut, pretend life
is just dandy. We forget our place and
move toward a future where one gets past
the present. All these parochial things,
salvations that have kept us all insane
are washed up on our shores. Creature comforts
float about the lapping waves, the skinny
legs of fledgling gulls and five sandpipers.
It is time to heal, my loves. Forgive us,
Elders. I know you speak the truth. We are
the land, and we undo our very selves.
Microscopic truths, are profoundly hard
to see. The plastic is in the water-
ways. Our plastic is in the animals.
Plastic is in our bloodstreams. It is time
to heal, my loves, before we give up hope
to the heavens, and a sea of red dust
above. Yes, we found a planet. It is
far from being here. Our hands must become
the earth. The future stands upon what we
do now. There's time to heal what we have left,
to plant trees, sow seeds, revel in the green,
leave the oceans to themselves. It is time
to heal, my loves, so we don't lose it all.

John Robert Grogan

The tears of Mazus radicans

Or, *stopping to chat to the flower at the side of the track*

i stop to chat to the flower at the side of the track . she says notice the shadows not the light . i say why . my feet are sore . she says but the dead are crying . can you not feel them through your roots . can you hear them . they say to walk in the clouds . i say it is too light up there . she says look up . can you not see the giant . she is sleeping . she wants you to scratch her back . she is lazy so it is up to you . i say my feet are sore . i am looking at you . you look like an angel . she says let the pain shine . wear it on your skin . i say i . i saw you because of the shadows . she says you're not the only one growing old . i see the giant . i feel the dead . i have tears in my throat from singing

Gail Ingram

After all

If I tell you before I go
that it's coming, like it always
has arrived, about the same time
you first realise the air is laden,
cautionary, and the wild trumpets
are not made of gold, that the birds
are absconding in their millions

If I tell you, what will you think,
my knowledge between your brows,
angry voices from the street
falling to outrage, egos of mounting control
scrambling for ascendancy;
will you act even then, even then,
as loudspeakers blare, calling your number.

Linda Stevenson

Enough rope to hang us all

Dazzling blue brutality   we all pray for rain
pollies and cameras head west   another sound bite juggernaut
as if election campaigns never end
or trite phrases assuage despair while a river system dies

each side pledges help   slice the pie differently vs cut the surplus
bulwark seats get handouts but there's no relief to a basin's thirst
elsewhere Pangea soils blow away   shroud sun
and cloak fleeces yet to be shorn 600 km south

on TV a farmer drops the stoic mask   admits *it's me or the property*
he is the fraying end of a thin white rope that's tied this land
to practices at odds with capacity
he'll take that mindset to coastal paddocks where rains still fall

hubris and intransigence are in our DNA
all those Anglo-Celtic émigrés who survived
second sons of lesser gentry who served Empire
urban poor purged from the slums of London
for stealing bread
tenant farmers strong enough to walk out of Ireland
after the blight

Tory lords leveraged that crisis to clear 'lazy' labourers
from 'their' valuable holdings
there's an air of déjà vu about the once-lucky country
our government procrastinates on climate action
ignoring 65,000-plus years of traditional knowledge
that sustained the greatest estate
popular memory denies we rode to prosperity

not only on the sheep's back
but that of our First Peoples' unpaid labour   yet their Voice is
unwelcome in the people's house while treaty's a concept
a shouty media doesn't want quiet Australians to consider

Europeans couldn't see the delicate balance of life
on this island continent
wouldn't bear heavy hooves, land clearing, and illegal dams
in a blip of geological time so-fragile soil pods shattered in
the sedimentary layers of a once-inland sea

as New England dieback makes totems of shade trees
in eroding paddocks
and salty groundwater percolates out of riparian zones
cleared of filtering roots
developments on flood plains consume nature's food bowl
the black loam Lachlan Macquarie relied on to feed
the fledgling colony

this drought could be the fifth act   of our national tragedy
believe preachers of economic salvation
at your own peril
someone will always make a buck from the suffering of others

an undeclared climate emergency offers the powerful
with robotic miners
more opportunity to extract more from an emptied land
once communities and farming families flee
given our nation's heartless response to others, should we
become climate refugees—who would take us in?

Linda Adair

dad said

a tanka prose

He's a sixth generation broad-acre cocky.
Crop country dirt runs in his veins. His harvests, bags of grain per acre, are legendary.
Local growers revere him as some sort of rainmaker; sniffing the wind dad knows when the weather will change.

The drought will break, my dad said.

winter dusk
a blood sunset
across the sky—
feeling for warmth
in your last goodbye

Marilyn Humbert

Meat display

His woodblock is a sawn,
unvarnished chunk of tree trunk.
His cleaver, honed steel.
Its handle, an afterthought.

He's hacked through countless limbs,
binned bags of bone fragments,
rendered and stockpiled lard in vats.

To him farm animals
are bereft of sentience.
It's not deliberate cruelty,
just repetition's blindness.

In the street some stand and salivate
at the meat window display.
Sausages dripping and coiled
like the viscera that encases them.

You wrestle with your conscience
before walking in
and request a chopped heap
of something which once breathed.

Mark Mahemoff

DBX

(Beyond possible)

High white spaces cup in massive
architecture, light that roams untethered
from its source. Light without dazzle,
color or heat, uplifting, unpressing us,
almost caressing us, holiness commerce
has promised to bless us with—

out there the sun would kill us we know.
Would sizzle our jet-lagged, caffeinated flesh,
like the eggs they'd crack on the tarmac
back in Melbourne's Fahrenheit days.
Or do what it does to sheep in parallel animal
transit zones, penned in the hell we dreamt of
for them, in our small-town colonial way.

Past plastic palm trees, water fountains,
camel loads of perfume for Diwali,
past columns ringed with real gold,
and white-tiled temples of ablution,
we roll our trolleys on—

at the end of Terminal Three,
a toddler has broken free,
its laughter skylarks into the dome
where falcons used to be,

and vacant as a passenger's mind
the air-conditioned air
cannot remember where
it came from in the light, out there
the planes are taking on supplies—

and if all the jets stopped bombing Yemen,
if the sheep could breathe and the men in white
never did what they did to Khashoggi,
beyond possible could mean something more
than age-old certainties, could be another
answer for the small still voice, forever
asking the same question; an oasis, say,
for desert-dwellers, with shade and
ample water for their flocks.

Matina Doumos

The phrase *beyond possible* is sourced from an advertising slogan for Dubai

Modern words

These words materialise
en masse from all manner
of mouths & media.

The public lexicon
contracts & expands
rhythmically,

changing with #culturaltrends,
with advances in
science

&
tech
-nology.
Word clouds
of set sizes & shapes
form amidst the greenhouse
gases of our polluted atmosphere.

Our future is   skywritten
—written not in those   constellations
                    of distant, glittering suns

but in our own   atmosphere,
in those shifting   cloudscapes
and our own   SUN.

Meteorology is the modern, evidence-based astrology.

How could the words be misread
by so many for so long?

Maybe this has little to do with literacy
yet a great deal to do with the fact

that, as our globe warmed,

the American Dialect Society's
Word of the Year
changed marginally
from 'truthiness' in 2005
to 'fake news' in 2017.

That 2016
Oxford Word of the Year
—'post-truth'—
rings true

like an alarm bell
some are deaf to.

Michael J Leach

Causality

The tideline, a scar of fishing hooks, cigarette butts and broken plastic.
My toe bleeds when it moves across the sharp break of a bottle
that once held water, and its parts now mingle with the greater blue.
An offering to the deep. Minute shards find a home everywhere.
Microplastics float into the mouths of zooplankton, into fish, into us.
All flesh infused with it. Wading into the shallows, I drop to my knees
in the soft sand. I cup my palms to show gratitude. A brisk wave slaps
my face.

Rosanna E Licari

The cemetery bats

Some want you gone. They fear your vampire links; your
blackened claws like lacquered question marks. Clinging
high above the sarsaparilla and native frangipani, beyond
the ancient echoes of paperbark canoes, tall bloodwoods
drip as russet mantles twist and swing like graceless
acrobats. Glassy amber eyes reflect in honeyed melaleuca:
fruity mounds rise up—occupied with latent life—among
the long or freshly dead, who,
lying silent, unperturbed, re-join their role
in life's repeating fractal forms.
Not all who see our fruit bat's sky-assault marvel
at their number or persistence. Funky rain-day
stink, ruined washing and purple stains on little Ruby's pricey
trampoline drown out chiroptera's keystone species claim.
After the daisies and hibiscus have gone to bed, dark hail
alive with shriek and fur shadows Ocean Drive. I stay outside
rejoicing in this wondrous sight. I raise my mango daquiri and toast
all future journeys of Bram Stoker's pollinating revellers
as they commence their sonic evening dance.

Lorraine Gibson

Fishing

asphalt's thick dark skin
peeled apart

hydro excavation they call it
cut & suck

a huddle of backs
sink the line deep

past rooted fingers
cables of light & power

string one blank face   to another
beads on a thread

hold one end tight
even as cat-gut sears

the hook is sharp
not cow or whale bone

shimmer of iron
ore re-made

its teeth glimmer
where Papatūānuku swims

bite
her rich, loamy flesh

it'll hold, they cry
she's a beauty

reel her in
heads high & legs wide

slap   hands on back
her threshing tail, breaks

the surface, mouth wide
gasping for breath

Rachel Smith

When an owl dies

Today the weather is so hot it's no longer shocking. Air is thick with un-formed rain until it rains, and every wet stone set, and leaf left, rocks with moss, mould, in mud, flood, good down-pour to forest floor, the toad-road south clogged with spawned brood. Window frames in our falling down cottage are held together with spider web, wound tight, sticky in the damp heat, holding us to this place, this mountain.

My mountain is always in my view, even as I circle the foothills thinking I am travelling away, all I am doing is circling. It's something that should be known when I put all my faith to work to move this particular mountain. It disturbs my horizon, stands preening, blocking my sunrise. It will never come to me. I am always the supplicant, even though I know my place, challenging it to accept my climb. I can name and name, in language after language—
fell ben massif jebel peak alp mont gunung cordillera sierra montaine. It is my naming, given to the indifferent mountain to make an unlikely claim of knowing—never the mountain relinquishing its name to me… Hindu Kush, Kosciuszko, Kinyeti, Deriba, Caldera Pidurutalagala, Puncak Jaya

Walking towards my mountain, through the stubble of last season's oats, a following of swallows picks disturbed insects from yellowing grass. Welcome swallows…

The dead owl lies on a floor of pine needles, aura gone as life left, but in an aureole of feathers, brown and grey, speckled and barred.

Barn Owl, a soft, unassuming body, given emphasis by the corona of its own dress from the death moult spread in a light night breeze. I hope it was flying under a full hunting moon when it died.

*

But how could I have forgotten this? On this day, in this year, one million species face extinction. The human drive for expansion, development, wanting more instead of enough, is enough to point a finger and cast blame on us. We can pull in Nietzsche here and an existential argument for why we should not perish with all the rest, but when resentment becomes a creative force for revenge and justice, and if we're weighing actions on a scale of good and evil, and when we think that if we name something we own it, we could use this philosophy of plenty-as-not-enough as a psychology of blame.

It may have been a hunting moon, but, equally, it may have been a hunger moon, that did for my owl on this mountain. Either way, my owl is lost.

Sandra Renew

Unhooking the lip

for Courtney Sina Meredith

She cups my name in her hands
like an undersized fish, unhooks

his lip, slips him back into shoals
beneath our feet that'll eddy him off

to someplace beyond reach. She invites
me to close my eyes in this too-bright

room where there is no running
water or waxing moon. I hear it weir

across rocks, vortex in my ears: her voice
is a raised hand out of the rip, as if to signal

drowning yet guides me until we're neck-deep
She asks who I think about when I picture

the ocean. I trace his voice, watch his face float
to the surface. She curls a phrase, *Ka kite ano*

on the sandbank, presses a mask to my mouth
We wade out to the wreck, peer through

cracked glass, shine a light into the belly
of his demise. She brushes my hand over

a new fish, mouths something I miss
Stroke its gills as I feel a tail thrill against

my wrist. When I open my eyes, she holds
the hook. There is blood on the line.

Sean West

Ka kite ano is a Māori phrase for 'until I see you again.'

Pillage

Rip me
like an open-cut mine
a bloody iron ore mess
feed me the milk
of tailing ponds
yellowcake the pillow
for my head.

Fell me
like a wood chip forest
inhale their final breath.

Cultivate me
in the open field
until salt rises
from my eyes.

Burn me
like the end of time
flames
melt the planet's ice.

Drain me
like a desert well
brimming for thousands
of years.

Teach me
the world
is rightfully mine
my actions
pay no price.

Raise me
like a plastic island
floating out at sea,
the creatures
rotting in the depths
have nothing
to do with me.

Yes, rip me,
like an open-cut mine
hold me to your chest
a radioactive baby
suckling
the highly toxic breast.

Shaine Melrose

Night vision
(abridged version)

A moth sets out on the path
following the gentle calling
of celestial light
transverse orientation leaves her
circumnavigating a man-made moon
on a back porch
round and round
perception of time and space
disintegrating along with
her inner night sky.

A man commutes home
sense of place
in the milky way obscured
but 'day' done in the office
long after the sun sunk
below the horizon
he toiled on
until streetlights
became his northern stars
guiding him home
but farther away
from himself.

A blackout hits
we only notice our reliance
on perpetual illumination
when the switch no longer
lights up our entire lives
keeping at bay the fear
of our own darkness.
A powerline fault
is the culprit—

disruption in the artificial arteries
we've spread across the land
to sustain us
wildfire now raging
burning
like a moth to flame
the obsession
now a burden.

A sea turtle
loses trace of moonlight
reflected off wave tops
his ancient navigation system
superseded by the allure
of a high rise—
beacon of blue light
keeping him from
journeying safely out to sea.

A girl lights a candle
turns off her phone
welcomes the shadows
in search of reclaiming
her own delicate bio rhythms—
the internal clock
as she closes her account
of sleep debt
and lets her senses remember
the potency of her own
night vision.

Stacey Cotter Manière

Survivalist

It became a trip marker in the crackle of cane fields,
a sign that the beach was not far now.
Buildings of dusty, unchanging carob,
low-slung and windowless,
wind turbines blurring,
a fraying ensign knotted by wind.
All those years of passing by, never any sign of life.

We imagined a dark bunker,
its sacks of dried legumes,
tinned tuna, treacle,
jerrycans of kero and diesel,
ampoules of penicillin,
and for later, seed packets, de-sal rigs,
ammo and oiled rifles
mummified in canvas shrouds.

Our girls have grown, have their own holiday plans.
Last summer we drove west, alone,
across the black-soil plains in locust season,
arriving with an almost clean windscreen.

An actuary would say my chances are good
of outliving the last koala.

Our daughters have no children.

Penelope Layland

Thousands of years

Fire rims the town. Atop the hill we watch.
The rains have not come. The ground is baked hard.
Long horned cattle thin, the boys who watch them

Skin stretched on bones, like the women with wood,
For cooking, balanced on their heads, harder
To find, further to walk, more energy—

Less food. For thousands of years, the Elders
Knew in which week to plant the seeds, the stars
Showed them; the universe, the world, in order.

Sitting around the campfire in the night
Looking into the distance and the dark,
The future may not be a place they go.

Ruth Nelson

Chromesthesia

Still inexplicably fulgent
something you might aspire to

sound is lurid red, white staccato
amanita muscaria whispers 'eat me'

your fingers brush the cap
find a message in braille
you sort of understand
but cannot explain

it's of the gut, the heart
the internal organs
can't be transmitted or owned
green pinwheels and lilac-violet
cortinarius archeri
sings a siren song
directly into your head.

You want to taste the voice
your body opening
to buzz and shift.

You know these spaces
the microbes that colonise
your body, lean into the gap
as if it were home

not the one you grew up in
scratching on the record player
of faulty love, the skyscrapers
that thrashed you
into someone else's shape
you continue to fight
with breath and light

the one you have to grow into
body broken open
rebuilding itself
molecules to structures
a new strain
scent rotting and sweet
sorrowful and exquisite
as deep pine green.

Magdalena Ball

INSCRIBING OUR DESTINY

'Mid-July. An autumn leaf clings to a twig.'

Amanda Anastasi

'another year
slips through my fingers
like sand ....'

—This weight I hold, *Michelle Brock*

'the mind is the Earth is the mind.'

—Waxing moon in Virgo, *Ivy Ireland*

'this is the beginning
—not the end.'

—We borrow from the future, *Alicia Sometimes*

Waxing moon in Virgo

Lone magpie cry against morning.
Sometimes you implode inside to experience it:
galaxy upon galaxy of no new Earth,
all alone against the colossal empty.

You think *colossal empty* and are proud of it,
as though the real fears could be quantified,
and, once named, obliterated by word-magic—
as though dying to it all was ever enough.

Dying is enough, yet you refute the finer points,
so this forfeiture continues.

This one is dying, this old Earth you loved,
part of you dares it to go.
Part of you must have sent it packing:
the mind is the Earth is the mind.

Grinning, because even in the leather of all this ending,
the animal continues, the *colossal empty* still grants boons;
magpie song still drowns out the tick of continuing,
sunrise still enters with black tea. Perhaps ginger.

Ivy Ireland

Tanka for the planet

counting the ways earth
replies groaning, sweating, shocked
dismay, wild yet still
waiting for gouging to stop
dreaming of new ways and paths

hearing songs from wind
overtures blocked out in fear
uncomfortable
leaving barren arias
replacing fruitful song lines

learning those stories
mapped out by ancients seeing
earth's bounty as gifts
finding signs in each season
steering possible harvests

moulting spider crabs
owls puzzling over change
tigers roaming wild
where lands once coupled in grand
design, yet there is time still

realising boldly
ways to halt new violence
earth over-fished, grazed
cropped, monopolies focus
cash profit, blind to planet,

calling out once more
look long term, consider plans
to stop late warming, grow green
in far denuded landscapes
remembering our partners

discovering new
birdsong where forest bushland
was felled for man,
kind once more considering
planet beyond tomorrow

shining, once icy
painted stories relating
encounters on earth
existing in virgin space
this blue dot seen from far off

Adèle Ogiér Jones

Capitalism and jellyfish on the shore

I

The impact of the dingo fence is seen
From space. Satellites silent witnesses
To the loss of vegetation. The mobs

Of kangaroos no longer kept in check.
Lake Menindee looks like a desert, the
Sand an expanse on which my children run.

The water minister changes the rules to
Allow floodplain harvesting, slaughtering
The river system. People look away.

In the city, we debate climate change.
Journalists ask me questions about mental health.
Wearing our masks, we argue about death.

II

Jellyfish are taking over the world
Said the headline. Oxygen levels have
Dropped by 2%, the temperature is

Up by .9 degrees Celsius and
We ate their predators. We ate them up.
At the surface, capitalism lies

Washed up on a beach. Murdoch pushes its
Corpse across the sand, spraying its gases
On the children demanding survival.

Once upon a time, the ecosystems
Of the world were on the brink of collapse.
A point of singularity. Unknown.

Ruth Nelson

In the next galaxy

after Ruth Stone

No one is looking at
their phones.
Technology is obsolete.
Children are schooled
in mental telepathy.
They beam the green laser
of their attention and listen
to the trees grow.
Trees: their primary tutors.
Whales: their worship.
Back here, we float
on top of our debris, gadgets
lashed together with fishing line.
While in the next galaxy,
they sigh contented, at home
in their fourth dimensional cottages
which none of us can see.

Laura Jan Shore

The privilege of a Wardian case

Glass can distort
I see shadows
Is that your silhouette
that brief untouched passing

Our Wardian case
balances on the oceans edge
We are *exquisite apart*
warding the world
scanner codes hexes
etched on doors gateways
magic symbols
that fade with time

A world beyond half hidden
half too clearly seen
ricochets around us
We chart trajectories
of flying shrapnel
test toughened glass
predict fractures

A domed city
on a hostile planet
last loneliest
the daily wait for the breached seal
the hiss of a noxious leak

I look out through cloudy glass
at passing brights and darks
Second-hand lives
mediated through panes
flickering pixels of the real
we stay alive but do not dance

Alexandra Fraser

The Wardian case (invented by Nathanial Ward, nineteenth century): a glass-sided airtight case which formed a sealed protective enclosure, or vivarium, for keeping living things under semi-natural controlled environmental conditions for their survival and for observation.

Italicised phrases refer to Auckland, originating in Rudyard Kipling's poem, 'The song of the cities'.

We borrow from the future

lines move

invisible bands shift
populations. We have split
in two. Creeping upwards
to the Northern Hemisphere and further downwards
past the low reaches of the south. We are widening
this weave. Wrenching liveable spaces out from the hands
of others. Every day we pull at this thread—tearing it from the centre
dragging it, stretching it until it frays

Surging temperatures, sun-baked rainfall patterns
flaming spread of Ross River and other viruses
mobilising to new areas. Malaria and dengue advance
incubators of mosquito species breeding in saltwater—
settling homes closer to broader populations. Brittle biodiversity

receding. Rats and other rodents flourishing—pliable to the decaying
surrounds. They know how to best live among people
Pathogens from animals increase as the line swells
A loss of predators mean many roam with
consequence. Some fall into extinction, others thrive
Variations seesawing, tipping over balance   to one side

the lines shadow over angle-stemmed myrtle
a worn shawl of rubbish thrown atop of them
cleared-out land of the black-flanked rock-wallaby
nesting sites of sea turtles vulnerable to high sea-level
endless lists of unknown reverberations

We grasp the weight of relocation
dirtier air smudging our airspace
        warmer oceans and parched earth sear
our topography: drought-scapes scattered across continents
        fires crawling into rainforests and camping out

We know this is not just about extremes
        but also, everything in between:
drinking water, hygiene, social structures, connection
how we embrace science and the wisdom of elders
how we walk along the dirt and shoreline with purpose

this is the beginning
                —not the end

We continue displacing these lines. Careening
them past escapable deadlines without halting

        we clutch this climate band, sweating
        and heaving as we hold on tight
        extending and elongating
areas of unreliable weather
                scorched soil and weeping trees

                We must draw the line
in the sand and sea and air and ground

stop splitting ourselves in two
live as one for this unravelling planet

and stitch back every single thread.

Alicia Sometimes

departures, arrivals

Airport of the future. Devoid of take-offs, landings. Derelict hub; remnant of the passenger era. Heat of steel, glass. Kids barefoot on tarmac. The encampments were quick to spread here. Spaces once open. Signs no longer apply. Arrows lead to nothings, nowheres. Proliferation of tents, tarps, improvs on a theme of shelter. 'Temporary' uttered less and less (palliative word). Fires cast the only night-lighting. The last of the dogs, howling for the gone. A thinning-out. Sustenance amounts to sprouts in water. Seeds once saved. Harvesting water from the slants of roofs. A hangar becomes hothouse, an airliner becomes home. Hierarchies, too, are grounded (why refuel them?). Travel is but a story. The endless elsewhere. What was once a city's most complex intersection (flightpath web). That ancient theme of waiting.

Stu Hatton

Proposed highway

A woman notes the mark on a lake's measuring post.
A man lets his dog off the leash
and, as it drinks, a group of fowl retreat
in the tannin water.
On a whim he asks her about the highway
that would part these wetlands:
        there would be two lakes, still, but divorced somehow;
        it would affect the system's integrity, the crossflow.
Like some Cartesian rift—mind
from body—
        a broken shadow
we take everywhere.

Sunny Wignall

Black fella—white fella

White fella—I see you
Long ago, my ancestors saw your ancestors arrive
They came ashore at this cove; many were barely alive
Mine did not know that yours did not want to be in our land
But your legal system is something I now understand
I now know your ancestors were sent here in prison ships
According to laws that were issued from your leaders' lips
Half way across the world your ancestors were forced to roam
Seeking comfort in things they were accustomed to from home
They brought with them creatures my ancestors had never known
And destroyed the creatures around which our culture had grown

Black fella—I see you—I hear you
When my ancestors were unloaded upon this strange shore
They did not know your language or your traditional lore
My people did not know that your people managed the land
Your culture and ecology, mine did not understand
My people's leaders said yours were not civilised like us
They said yours did not own the land; it's *terra nullius*
So my people came, and took all of the land that they saw
Then they told you that possession is nine-tenths of the law
But I now know that in this case our possession is theft
And losing access to country left your people bereft
Your people were forbidden from speaking in their own tongue
And your traditional songs were not allowed to be sung
Your families and societies were torn asunder
Because my ancestors came here, to this land down under
I see that it's many of your people who are now poor
It is your people who are locked up, as mine were before
Your people were stolen, imprisoned, enslaved, raped, and killed
So that my ancestors' aspirations could be fulfilled

Black fella—I see you—I hear you
My people brought a foreign agriculture when they came
And they took whatever they could, when they hunted your game
With the grazing of their sheep, they destroyed your murnong fields
That no longer grow in abundance nor produce great yields
My people brought in sheep and cattle, the rabbit, the fox
And cut down the gums, ironbarks, red cedar, pines, and box
The soils have been carried away by the water and wind
Against this country my people have so surely sinned
I am so ashamed of this. What must your ancestors think?
These changes my people made, they drove your totems extinct
Thylacine, paradise parrot, desert rat-kangaroo
Lesser bilby, desert bandicoot, broad-faced potoroo
This land's ecology we are starting to understand
But alas, my people are still strangers here in this land
Because I still know so little of your language and lore
There is much that I can learn, if I listen to you more
For this to happen, our leaders will have to make a choice
To hear First Nations perspectives; hear a First Nations Voice

White fella—I see you—I hear you
We have so much to learn if we listen to each other
We can heal country if you regard me as your brother
Yallara, walilya and moda can never return
But if we can work together I know that we can learn
To care for country better than we ever have before
By using both your science and our traditional lore
If we work together there is so much that we can gain
If we walk arm in arm we can both be free of our pain
But for us to make our journey forward together last
We must share with all Australians, the truth of our past

Andrew Hingston

Persistence

Waking, I twiddle digital knobs
tweaking O_2 levels
air-conditioning floods
my sky-reaching home with
breathable levels of this rare gas.

Rising from hyperbaric chamber
blinds automatically open upon
concrete-covered landscape;
once flourishing forests
razed memories.

I swallow a tablet
cringing at bitterness;
water recycled from waste
the only consumable liquid
remaining.

Via holographic display
my son boasts of
cybernetic augmentation
replacement for failing organs;
human touch a vague dream.

For the drive to work
I don full body suit
its reflective surfaces
protection against
instant sunburn.

Sulphuric mist
fills the atmosphere
toxic gases kill.
virulent viruses
the dominant lifeform.

Depressurised at work
I operate digital console
manoeuvring robotic drills
closing in on Earth's core
the last untapped resource.

When darkness falls
I retire to hyperbaric chamber
this womb of protection
humanity's final defence
against past negligence.

AR Levett

An ecology of healing

Anthropocene defeating
Indigenous nations rise, back up
Barren lands reinitiate
Nullifying *terra nullius*, nutritious firestick reignition
Ancient agricultural systems recognition
Magical ecological intuitions rekindled

Planetary business rebalancing scales
Rainbow Snake swallowing *bolung*,
regurgitating Earth with water
Dry to wet, head to tail fertilisation of saline soil
Re-coralising barriered sadness
On the boundaries of civilisation

Reharmonising, resynchronising moon tides
In time with ecological rhythms
Rebirth from ancestral womb
Blood-life source, cosmic strength inner force:
Rains fall, seasons change, animals multiply
To the power of infinitesimal cyclical renewal

When ecology is at risk
Karadjeri let blood flow red
Fertilising parrot fish
Brings success in hunting, gathering
Observance of own-kill rules
Ensuring plentiful supplies of food
Myth ritual totemism inseparable unity principle
Collective symbolic actions realised

To find answers, we return to a place before the beginning
In our minds moving forth back in time ceremony:
gamil-bidiwii epistemology
Healing scarred tree pedagogy
Kamilaroi stories of preservation
passed down to cultural custodians
generation to generation
Memic immortality seen, heard in the rippling rings of trees
Carved stories, documents, charted time immemorial
Ancient symbols sing and dance: *Kubbaanjhaan*
Bloodlines flow through landscapes sustaining life

We chant as we carve,
One ochred body, entranced
Reciting stories, protecting
Opening the genetic memory of responsibility
Collective consciousness, recreation of DNA's
double-helix umbilical cords
pulling mind's heart connecting Country
Carved stories, sharpened tools honed on whetstone earth
Moving forth back Dreaming: *Burruguu-ngayi-li*
An ecology of healing
Anthropocene defeating.

Andrew Geoffrey Kwabena Moss

The days

On the first day planes stopped flying, birds began singing into the silence; ghosts inhabited the town

On the second day after the rain the rivers began flowing again, etching the land with green valleys

On the third day in the fishing village doors were kept tightly closed; boats knocked at the floating docks

On the fourth day grass grew through the cobblestones, up the walls of the houses choked the chimneys with green velvet, snug as a warm blanket; the windows in the houses stared blindly

On the fifth day the fishermen opened their doors, walked down to the harbour, cast their nets from their boats, pulled them in over the side, then hung them out to dry like cobwebs catching each dewdrop, used their knives on the rocks and every oyster delivered a pearl

On the sixth day the children abandoned their devices and followed the wind through the empty streets, danced into the mountains and played in the clear pools at the foot of waterfalls, while back in the village their parents waited for the sacred lotus to rise into sunlight

On the seventh day the children came home, the wind swept through each open door the world began to breathe and the fishermen saw that it was good for the earth had rested…

Gail Hennessy

Afterlife

inspired by *The Oil Drums* by Jeffrey Smart

I think of Exxon Valdez, Deepwater Horizon.
The glossy public face – its formal geometry

Of slick colour and the artist's golden ratio –
Vivid as a kelp garden teeming with life in the

Bight where they want to drill: cyan, cadmium,
The shrill yellow of unblackened coral, texture

Smooth as honeyed trumpet music. A mastaba
Of greed, a historical set piece, a burning afterlife.

Jane Frank

design

The world is a corpse-eater—Gospel of Phillip

hesitant mauve against final cause red. jacaranda bows to the flame tree. sea hawk powers past. dog moans somewhere distant. dry wind cuts through dead snake grass. the cosmological decisiveness acquiesces to give you a seat in the scene. instead you rise.

you rise. too tardy for proper courtesy. introduce terms like teleological uncertainty to the morning. feel bad about it. continue on regardless. whims like intelligent design seep from the landscape. you roll your eyes. thread your toes through the pre-crushed petals. bleed more red. mauve deserves to be ignored. too reminiscent of society ladies.

camphor laurels are society ladies. they loom out there. nodding heads at fashionable dinners. chickens bob about in their run. they have not had breakfast. you have not had breakfast nor have you kissed your lover's forehead for days. the ocean you can barely see is out there anyway. constantly gobbling up shore. discretely so you barely notice. it is edging closer.

every day I realise we've left it too late to get it back, but then I work like a bitch to get it back. speaks a bush regeneration agent in the new day air. but you are scribbling. too busy for Sisyphus. lines turn into letters turn into denials you will never send. lack denotes longing. admission of longing assumes a fault somewhere. fault leads itself right down the garden path to blame.

there are billions upon billions of parallel worlds reclining just through that mauve and red. bathing just beyond that powdered baby blue and new leaf green. colours are veils. there are other worlds. just there on that other side. just get to them. just go. just get to one.

Ivy Ireland

Auguries drawn from an empty glass

The future is yellow and full of gods
dried wheat plains   fulvid hills

yellowing carcasses sun-stroked
            bleached out pale straw bones

stained streams choked
            wind dry to the never sea

clay cliffs stand against
            an ocean of ochre sand
            below saffron cloud sky

and everywhere sound calls   bleats for rescue
pattered prayers   directionless
focused   in vain

fed on faltering speech small gods evolve
            grow golden
impervious   unmoved

they are enthroned in high palanquins
gauded with turquoise   lapis   aquamarine

they are heavy on our shoulders
            we stumble on

feet raising clouds of yellow dust   and heads full
of longing   for our lost world and for

the crystal chink of ice
            in our own glass

Alexandra Fraser

Prohoros—in the Cave of the Apocalypse

Apocrypha

In bitter, brittle, wind-honed light
the sage's searing visions come:
'There shall be teeming multitudes of men
where once were flocks and herds,
birds and beasts and creatures of the seas;
men shall be as pestilence and locusts
to the fragile earth, consuming all
voraciously, stripping the ample granary,
so that the birds take flight, alarmed,
wretched beasts retreat in fear, trees
like phantoms wither at the roots, then
disappear. The crystal seas shall putrefy
with sudden death, their wondrous creatures,
miracles of God's delight—blithe dolphins
and shy seahorses—will atrophy, when
the sun's eye, magnified, unrelenting
in its might, shall gather overpowering
intensity, and perish all—
Thus shall we witness what God's hand
has wrought—'

My master burned
with brimstone of his prophecies,
the ague of his visions and their awesome
might, and in the fitful, wintry light,
familiars cowered at his side, spirits

of the wounded earth, racked by impending
terror. I nursed these portents in my soul
but did not write. My avatar, that old,
frail saint inhabited by tragedy, who spoke
in tongues of God's wrath and God's mercy,
bestowed upon his humble scribe,
rewarding faithful hands and mind,
the secrets of his heart and eyes,
gifts of the second sight.

Jena Woodhouse

Prohoros was the amanuensis (scribe) who transcribed the apocalyptic vision experienced in a cave on the island of Patmos (Greece) by St John the Divine, which became The Book of Revelation.

240 grams

Research Lab, Lord Howe Island, August 2018

Inside, I sort through a tide line, poured into a bucket
searching for nurdles in brown detritus mostly organic,
find soft brown globes, small air bladders, most with stems,
Colours are best, I can't detect the plastic transparencies.

Outside, I weigh a pendulous shape, a defrosted shearwater,
the drama needing much more weight. I measure the wing,
a wonder structure never put to use skimming the ocean
or soaring in the ballet of courtship, living life to the full.

This chick clawed its way out of a dark burrow
two metres underground and died in the blinding light.
I use callipers on the bill then start enthusiastically plucking
its belly, feeding a garden pillow fight, feathers flying.

I thrust some into a small plastic bag noting details
for chemical testing. The steel blade cuts into the skin
but being too gentle, unused to this work, I slice
through the connective tissue again and again, struggling

to find the stomach sac amongst the dense architecture.
It's empty, easy to miss. I push aside the glistening worminess,
the moist earthiness we share, cold nests inside instead of warmth.
The ropey intestine breeds distant cousins we have commandeered.

Our other half, the world within our world sharing our deep history
of symbiosis deserving nourishment, thousands of species inside
and outside, outnumbering our own body's cells. Meanwhile
tissue, fat and blood wedge intimately under my nails.

I carve the nuggety gizzard, peel back its border, open it out
like a fig revealing small black thorns (cuttlefish beaks), separate
the microplastics piece by piece, discards of our cult, proof
our worship is reckless and that there are no islands anymore.

I slip them in a bag, but they stick to my fingers slippery with slime
favouring disgust over negligence. How to make out-of-sight manifest?
A window onto terra from my home 600 Ks due west, feeding
the Great Pacific Gyre, the anonymous centres and edges, the frag.

Cruelty can be ecstatic, forgetful or as casual as littering,
letting storm drains do their work, vomiting plastic into the sea
eroding to tiny then tinier farting phenols and phthalates.
Twentieth century anxieties are being revised and updated.

The sky blooms a beautiful weight of blue, an endemic
Currawong rows overhead flashing black and white,
the colours which reality once scoured to the horizon.
I find myself stroking the soft dark head without thinking.

John Bennett

'Seabirds are starving to death on the remote Lord Howe Island, a crew filming for the BBC One documentary *Drowning in Plastic* has revealed. Their stomachs were so full of plastic there was no room for food.' —Victoria Gill, 'Marine plastic: Hundreds of fragments in dead seabirds', BBC News, 23 June, 2018

O let them be left, wildness and wet—

from *Inversnaid*—Gerard Manley Hopkins

I am trying to keep my head
    above
but today elegies of
belugas retrieved from
Arctic floes
    sandbags over a crashing dam
quietly designed
to stem the rage
    of winter on the wane

So   what to do about puddle clay
short-lived lichen   the grey heron
nesting on terminal moraine in full stop
    the general thrusting

How to mourn
    drowned mountains
drowned spires visible only
    at low tide
    bells tolling intermittently
across the North Sea   / summoning/

Terracotta chimneys
from wasted villages
    wait   for the return

Last century /it surprises me to say/
my girlfriend's nightdress catches fire
/unlike a kingfisher/

her sculpted skin pink and glistening makes
new topographies neck to knee
She lifts her face away

What it takes
to keep the head above
rivers of mud

The way it is
oceans collide in terraced homes along sea roads
at the summit of high peaks

leaving a souvenir tree
disposable hearth /from Ikea/
exposed bones on the north face
of men and women in boots like Mallory

Julie Maclean

A climate of mortality meets Melbourne winter

who'll leave a cedilla to
compost
unwritten in stone

where old breathing
forests are gone to fossil
drives who'll

wonder if bacteria
can work
rock as caves were

painted in Lascaux or
if it happens that
the other were to think

as we who make books
of trees a potpourri
of matter who despite

the improbability
will hope
that we might not have

done this thing
and find
on a morning

crisp with winter sun
it's unimaginable all is not
well

who'll bookmark
a future that happened
yesterday

Anne Elvey

Subject to change

at the beach, two-magpies
carol a joyful report

all's well, nothing to fear
no swell, no wind

to stir the world
perfect now
                    less than perfect later

Moya Pacey

Tales of old

Our grandma tells us stories of what the world once was.
We listen in wonder as she whispers her tales of old.
Grandma's hair is wispy and grey; she has lived many a year;
But as she speaks of former Earth, her voice is steady and bold.

Grandma's bones are stiff, and they creak as she hobbles.
She grasps her wooden walking stick with trembling hands.
But when she speaks of the old world, a world of hope,
Her eyes shine with wonder as she remembers the lands.

She says when it rained, the air felt heavy and damp.
She says the rushing wind felt cool against her cheeks.
She says the sea was salty and went on for miles.
She says the mountains were majestic and had snowy peaks.

Grandma tells us of the creatures that once roamed Earth.
She says the lions were fierce and had a mighty roar.
She says below the ocean depths, whales glided along.
She says that through the cobalt skies, eagles would soar.

But these are only stories. Tales of long ago.
Now, the land is barren. Deserted and dry.
There are no more mountains. There is no more sea.
Plumes of dark smoke cloud the once brilliant sky.

Sometimes, Grandma scrunches her eyes tightly shut.
Salty tears trickle slowly down her wrinkly face.
We know she is remembering old life on Earth.
It must have been the most magnificent place…

The world was once a terrain of rolling hills and dewy grass,
Of skies filled with glittering stars and a moon so bright.
Now, we live in a wasteland of dry earth and yellow shrubs.
The skies are always dark. It is forever night.

Whenever Grandma tells us stories of the past,
She ends them by whispering softly into our ears…
'The world can only be changed if you are willing to change it.'
We are willing to change it. It's needed to change for years.

Kate Nicholas Edgar, 12 years

Rite of passage

It's considered a rite of passage
to stand beneath the sky
to venture forth from underground
if only for a while.

With breathing masks and goggles
and a robot for a guide
we walked upon a beach of bones
my fellow classmates and I.

Our eyes were drawn to the water
this vast expanse of sea
a wavering mass of oily black
and slimy pools of green.

Someone pointed skyward, where
through a gap in the greyish gloom
I saw a floating cloud of white
in a brilliant patch of blue.

It's considered a rite of passage
to stand beneath the sky
to mourn the passing of a world
if only for a while.

Garry Dean

Cliff

[Orithya] was blown off one of the cliffs hereabouts and met her death at the foot—Socrates.

The last time we walked this path it was there, and now it isn't.
What is left is beautifully coloured. I stare. But the old looks a ball-sack
heaped as it is. The nest we saw will be squashed
in the ruins. The doves have flown who knows where; I don't hear
a coo, do you? We look down together. Remnants
of pohutakawa salute the way the drowning are taught
to signal terror, before the event of course. We look up:
another fissure. This is bound to get worse before it gets better.

Rachel J Fenton

The Ministers

The Minister for Drought submits a proposal. *Due to the severity of the current situation, I propose a ban on external H_2O use, worldwide, with immediate effect.*

The Minister for Green Grass objects.

The Minister for the Sun supports his objection, stating he cannot sustain the portfolio of his colleague alone.

The Minister for Drought relents, caveats his proposal with *on grass excepted.*

The Minister for Fresh Air releases an audible sigh.

The Minister for Blue Sky clears his throat.

The Minister for Wind and the Minister for Solar exchange looks, having united since the Minister for Mining resigned.

The Minister for the Moon appears, he is rarely in attendance.

The Minister for Tides rises to his feet and continues to rise, pressure builds.

Order, order! cries the Minister for Earth, struggling to be heard.

JV Birch

Not drowning

after Mary Oliver

I knew the sea
had forgotten me, she
tumbled my body so forcefully, rippling
her silk skirts, her pockets
full of seaweed and sand. I sank
as I'd done before, lungs
bursting for air, nothing
beneath my feet and the cold maw of the deep,
but my prayers and they squirted
black as squid ink
diffusing on the waves. Somehow,
all muscle and sleek, the dolphins
circled, nuzzling close, lifting me. Somehow,
stroke by stroke, I ploughed through the surf, vestigial gills
revived, sprouting fins and a tail, I
returned again to where it all began
shyer, smaller, better.

Laura Jan Shore

Mooray

You wipe & wander
through a maze of trails stretched with webs as
though you were cutting a ribbon,
some official opening each few metres.

You stomp & wobble
through loud silence,
the cicada & whip
of corella light/
sky cut spear
of the Gymea lily, speckled
craze of Christmas bush in bloom.

You amble & stumble
till you reach a camp site, the
haphazard fireplace ringed with cans & stubbies,
some miniature Stonehenge.

Worn dirt, exorcised ash.
Tribal paint suggesting
Doug loves Linda
yet this scene
throbs with a history
of subtlety & excess.

I'll let any stranger
in on our people's tiny secret.

Between Big
Pineapples, Prawns & Rams we really
come to worship at the smaller,

hidden edge
where the weft of eucalypt scours the air,
its leaves stain ponds
to a sleepy tea that lulls us—
knowingly or not—

all to peace.

Les Wicks

The Revelation myth

When I return, after a long, forced exile, entering into the silence just after the storm. When I can splinter with my fingers the woodworm eaten ark laying in pieces in the street, where once as kids we fought together until the cleaved rib gave birth to our division; after all this, I'll tell them, finally, what I've seen.

I'll tell them how they set fires to deserts, razed mountains, bore holes through the sun. How boats with hidden eyes crossed horizons and tore through wave-breaks, hulls cringing, *heave-ho* and how they rounded the earth, tied chains to its circumference, packaged it up, boxed it, sectioned it, suffocated it, diminished it. And where their eyes were once are now gold pieces blinking in the light of dead stars a thousand, two thousand years old.

An eclipse of seagulls strain their wings against a late-summer sunset. A cascade of palm trees, a drowned oasis, a bent figure that appears, briefly, on the crest of a dune, against the sun outlining a crucifixion in silhouette. A murder of crows; a discarded, blood-smeared dagger partially obscured in the shifting sands like the mute Sphinx, like the pyramids at Giza that keep all the secrets we will never discover.

And I will tell them of the end first.

But I know they will not listen, not knowing in which direction to pray like a cracked-faced compass blind to its points. In the aftermath I lay in an empty room somewhere. Deep in the bellows of the house, a clock strikes midnight. A floorboard creaks underfoot. A man clears his throat. I wait for the handle to turn but only the broken spine of silence seeps under the door; for I know this to be impossible, for everyone is now gone. This many-roomed mansion fallen into disrepair, a dilapidated delirium of twisted shape and shadow.

The jaundiced skin of these walls I could slice with my sins. The moon feeds through its pale light and I write these final words in the blemished blue haze, knowing I shall never return, now that the sun is no longer so recognisable, nor so extraordinary.

And if I have one last wish, I would ask you to find a breach in the wall and to take me through to where the wind lives. Promise, you will take me to where the wind lives.

Lincoln Jaques

Before our Earth falls silent

While there are still trees along the avenue
a canopy of branches
their muted voices singing in the wires,
the giant eucalypt outside my window
an orchestra in the wind, I will walk through
the sunlight and shadow of the tree-tops

the softness of earth beneath
pretending it's all unchanged.
The black cockatoos preening each other's
beaks and feathers, like lovers, are gone
currawongs and warblers vanished.
I'd never longed for the wake-up call
of birdsong, until it ceased.

I will go back down to the bay
to swim among sea urchins and schools of fish
to marvel at rock pools at low tide
a water-garden of Earthly Delights
sea anemones and psychedelic nudibranch
strange mutants from an LSD trip gone wrong
as though already touched by chemical waste.

Giant crabs climb the rock-face
hide their rusting prehistoric bodies
from probing fingers,
entanglement of seaweed.

At twilight, moths come drifting
fall out of sight behind trees.
Blue fish flicker like gas flames
                    jump from your hands.

Margaret Bradstock

Double rainbow

A double rainbow arched over Leichhardt. Old and young alike looked up and smiled. It was the vision they'd been waiting for. Pessimists became optimists and optimists felt vindicated. Crime ceased. Cars slowed down or parked to watch. Everyone knew it would only last as long as rain and sunlight joined forces. Everyone's gaze was held by this vision. The promise of gold that had never been kept. And even as night came, long after it had disappeared, they all held the memory of what had occurred. There were small pools of hope left on every street.

Mark Mahemoff

This weight I hold

keep or kill
random acts of vengeance
in the firestorm . . .
beside a burnt-out house
a letterbox full of bills

at the dump
dozers and diggers argue
over spoils—
will these dinosaurs
inherit a plastic realm?

old-growth forest
the last mountain ash
cut down—
nothing now to brush
the clouds across the sky

Mars-tinged moon
bleeds across the evening sky
who will rise …
to dress the wounds
of our fractured world?

she runs to me
wave-washed and breeze-dried
sweet grandchild
with shells in her pockets
uncharted oceans in her eyes

another year
slips through my fingers
like sand …
this weight I hold
is her future

Michelle Brock

End of days

Vivid fossils
of an unknown species
of plant-eating dinosaurs,
preserved in grey–blue opal
rippled with turquoise tints,
were found beneath arid lands
once lush with vegetation
lagoons and rivers
flowing into the inland
Eromanga Sea

And I hope that when
the final cataclysm
destroys our unique planet,
my bones and yours,
buried deep underground
like the now-extinct dinosaurs,
will transmute over time
into fossilised opals
illuming the never-ending darkness

Colleen Z Burke

Fossilised bones discovered in an underground opal mine near Lightning Ridge, NSW, included remains of adult and juvenile dinosaurs, *Fostoria dhimbangunmal,* from the mid-Cretaceous period.

Decline

A tanka prose

The three longest rivers in Australia, the Murray, Darling, Murrumbidgee, their feeder creeks and many wetlands make up the Murray-Darling Basin. The original custodians, Aboriginal Nations managed this resource with respect. Taking only what they needed, fish, birds, animals, from the bush and forests through each season, during cycles of flood and drought.

tribes gather
dancing and singing
dreamtime stories
sharing the bounty
of the Basin

About 170 years ago white settlers arrived in search of new lands to make their own. Traditional owners were driven from their homelands. Resettled in missions and native settlements.

guns against
boomerang and spear
no contest …
'roos driven away
by sheep and cattle

New owners built dams and channel systems. Diverting water for farming and towns without understanding how the three great rivers are interconnected. Management is dependent on Federal and State powers.

algae blooms
clog
shrinking rivers
the stink
of dead fish

Combination of drought, changing rainfall patterns and too much water taken for farming and population needs has not been balance with the health of the rivers. The Basin's flora and fauna species are in decline. Many farmers and towns which rely on water from this vast system haven't received their allocations.

no answers
for communities—
politicians
blame each other
blame climate change

beside
a dry billabong
around the fire
voices chanting
beseeching spirits

full moon
this starry night
no cloud
casting shadows
on this dying land

Marilyn Humbert

The Murray-Darling Basin covers 1,059,000 square kms, 14% of Australia's land area. Less than 6% of the rainfall makes it into these slow flowing rivers: Murray-Darling Basin Authority

Water falls

I look at him in sleep, he rolls and sighs,
Blond curls askew, wet towels across the gaps
To slow the smoke that seeps inside our flat.

He cries. His mask with ducks is in the wash.
His face, so small, I try to hide my fear.
I birthed a child to see the end of days.

To see ahead, I look behind—they're there
In late warm sun, against the trees they dance.
We watched them dance, we young, they old, and all

The while, cascades of water fell, we'll find
Our souls again, dug deep into the ground
And life will come around, we will survive.

Ruth Nelson

After December; the summer in fog

A little black thing among the snow,
Crying 'weep! weep!' in notes of woe!
'Where are thy father and mother? say?'
'They are both gone up to the church to pray.'
—William Blake

When the mountains burn, the beaches wear mascara scars
And our soles become the charred carbon footprints of the promises
We gave ourselves. In the morning,
                        smoke peels through windowsills
And a slow wheeze comes from the baby monitor.
                                                Out in the forest,
The ghost gums have burnt and sent their silent souls howling into the air.
Now they walk the streets
                and make an urn of the suburbs.

My boys stand inside the door
                —barefoot supplicants to their lost selves
Hiding in the garden. The sky is finger-paint orange, a smudge of amber
And brown. We watch the future forming a graphite film on the deck
And wash it away as soot from our hands
                        —the country in its *coffin of black*
And Finn counting the cremated leaves falling on the lawn.
He asks about the animals,
                but places like Kyoto and Paris don't weigh the same

In his mind as the holocaust of flying foxes in the park;
                                                their little black wings
Like the tattered sails of storm-tossed yachts.
                        Here, we are trapped versions of ourselves,
Hemmed in by an After-Pay fate that has turned the air to dust and ash
And our lungs to a ravaged mirror of the world. A golden whistler
In the bottlebrush seems nature's soot stained warning bird
                        as an off-grey fog settles in the yard.
Time in the palm of our hands—fricative and restless,
                                        like children in the sullen night.

Peter Ramm

The climate at Wentworth Falls

after AR Ammons, & Charles Darwin in the Blue Mountains
for my kids & their families (who are also drawn to mountains)

I followed Darwin's Walk again this evening
to the falls,
from the ridgetop's open forest,
contouring
round the furrowed boughs of black ash
and the smooth pale stands
of peppermint and blue gum flaking
over banksia, mountain devil and waratah:

Zigzagging
down to the over-
cliff track where
clumps of button grass
and holly-like grevillea bloom
among the sedges of hanging swamps,
soils like peat collecting
along shales and sandstones,
the sponged seepage zones
of a fernery's rare collection:

And along to the lookout at the falls:

Here a bushfire haze still burnt
over the escarpment's western rim whilst drizzle
swirled around the fire tower
like a halo, an answered prayer pledging
to starve the conflagration of oxygen and heat:

But this change was forecast
to a rattled line of spoiling towns
threaded along the railway and Great Western Highway,
the length of a labyrinth's clear-felled, central ridge:

And while, after the rain, the blackened trees might once again
shoot green, the grasstrees fired
into flower, here
the industrial offering of sclerophyll is a knotty and wiry
garden of corpses
and pockets of virgin forest touched
for the very last time.

Phillip Hall

Options for a rogue species

(no particular order)

All-in nuclear war. An end to name-
calling, poking with toothpicks.
Backfiring surprise attack or not-so-
simple error. No Body Cares Department.
All quiet, post lethal shock treatment.
Million odd survivors wonder what in hell...
Gull way too ill to survey wasteland.

Not-so-benevolent global ruler,
super-entrepreturd seizes opp
to grab market for everything,
citing some god's shrill will.
(Of course it sounds familiar!)
Conformity equals sweet life with all
the discount candy floss you can eat.
Lion, imprisoned, thrown daily chicken.

A break-out of uncommon sense;
nationhoodlems morph into moral
citizens for good of all that's nature.
Beasts at their best saintly selves.
Improbable options must be aired.
Think dinosaurs, apes raising Cain.
Sunning lizard tongues a shiny fly.

Rogues continue to compete for things,
place crazy bids on Saturn's rings.
Madly consistent, domineering species
posts selfies on antisocial media even as
Mother Nature decides to destroy her own
creation with fire, flood, virus, CO_2
Relieved turtle enters sea, history.

Allan Lake

When the sun sets

Dreams wash up on a shoreline. Flotsam and jetsam thoughts, that only ever awaken hopes lost at sea. I am shipwrecked and so constantly alone on island in an ocean where the climatc of deceit was the only winner in the end. My island is sinking. The salted water has begun to lap against my feet. Dread, but I cannot step back or return to higher ground because there is none. My eyes search for signs amongst the broken vessels upon my arms. Sea birds cry accusingly, 'hu-man, you brought this upon thy self'. My longing has brought into my possession treasure chests filled with out-of-date mobiles, empty oil cans, broken toys and failed petrochems,' sunken airlines and forgotten 24-hour news networks. My fresh water is found in plastic bottles at the core beneath the dirt in the heart of the island. I knew deep beneath my downloads and virtual realities that something had to give. So, here I stand at the island's edge watching my world set. Tanned in cancer, overweight with regrets and filled with memories of things called snow and glaciers: It all melted away and turned the seas into oceans and oceans into vast deserts that washed away the sands of Arabian Nights. I am the only one here. The last of humanity. I am Sinbad with no one left to tell my tales.

Robert J Conlon

Ghosts on the moon path

This is not a travel story, but it tells you where my mind went and why my return is improbable. It could tell you why you should not listen to the shameful and appalling slagging off, incitement to violence, the roar and scream of big bikes leaving the pub down the road at closing time. Why a howling dog worrying about the moon is not alerting you that your gate may be a sanctuary. Why this lit cigarette dropped into a street bin will not light up the chocolate wrappers, cigarette packets, plastic cups, maps, instructions to pay, news bulletins on the missing, species extinguished, habitat mutilated.

Graves are crowded with room for water and every known ghost. Boats are crowded with welcoming ghosts. Their grave is water. Under water, moonlight crowds towards the grave.
Water rises to the moonpath.

They swim, die many deaths. The boat turns, rolls, hangs, sinks. Ghosts walk in crowds on the moonpath. Ghosts reminding us we are one blue planet, one mutually reliant humanity.

This is not a travel story. What is lost are our taut and tender tendencies, recovery moments—at the memorial for war, in a moon-lit dawn, one minute of silence bursting with birdsong.

Sandra Renew

Past perfect future indicative future tense

We'd kept string rolled into increasing balls
flattened and stored brown paper bags
folded butter-paper to line cake tins

filled the iron range with coal   baked bread
re-purposed worn woollen overcoats
into small woollen skirts

unravelled old jumpers knitted new
in multicoloured stripes
took jam sandwiches to school

listened to Rocky Starr Destination Venus
on the radio five o'clock Friday
our fifteen minutes of the future

we kept meat in an outdoor safe
wind blowing through the mesh
flies hovering

ninety-eight ninety-nine one hundred
coming ready or not
past my finger-tips the world changes
images fall past sunlit bones
through shadows of chance and choice
this way or that way   masked from us

we will play the fifteenth expansion of World of Warcraft
levelling up keeps us off the streets   our meals are delivered

the yellow dust thickens on our tents   rows of refuge   serried loss
when will our meals be delivered?   we remember hot buttered toast

our threads are showing   dressed in history's clothes
we are unravelled

we hoard paper   and in empty paddocks   harness
a lonely horse to a plough

I can breathe uncertainty
I can knit
I can unknot used string

Alexandra Fraser

Doubtless Sound

It's been a hundred years since the last newspaper collapsed, and seventy since the civil war that sealed us in this living tomb. When the *New York Times* shut its doors, people held bonfires in the streets. Or so they tell me. Nowadays, news travels via a sticky web of self-interested lies and misinformed speculation amongst the hiss and shunt and shudder of the machines. We work twelve hours a day, every day. One day I escape. No one has ever succeeded before. I crawl out of the vent, gasping for air. I stumble to my feet and raise my head. There is nothing, not a sound. Not a single tree or living creature. No birds or insects, no whisper of a freshening breeze. Endless dust and silence, utterly devoid. There is no hidden cloister of lucky-born living off our grinding bones and presiding over the churn of work and death. Only us and the machines. I return. Outside it's breathtaking—a prism of laughter and light and wind tripping through trees filled with rainbow-hued birds where our betters live idle and free. We'll meet this salvation one day. Or so I tell them.

Rebecca Douglas

Tabula rasa

Sixty harvests until the end of things,
until the last centaur folds from the fetlocks
beside his dry well,
till mermaids shed scales in dulling strips
and wallow in the tepid swell.
The phoenix cannot gather his scattered kindling
in such a wind.
The golden apple splits and turns wormy.
The sphinx has no riddle for the occasion.

The bright poppy, which grows best
in soil assaulted by flash flood or blood,
was no symbol of rebirth and morning, after all,
but a red flag of warning, semaphoring.

Sixty springs of diminishing returns,
then the last leviathan will lie bloated on the beach.
Gone, Gilgamesh, Bruegel's Babel, all of Beethoven,
angels twirling on the bright heads of pins.

Penelope Layland

Gulamany dreaming

High in the tree he gazed, alone,
at the dark and silent heath.
Studded with the white spires of dead gums.
Starved of water now, the forest was no more.
High in the tree, he had tasted, in the leaves,
the salt welling from the ground.
In hope, his coughing cry echoed around
but was met by silence, again.
He pulled at his skin, now loose and ragged on his bones,
and chewed on the handful of leaves left, sour in his mouth.
With one last glance at the emu stretched across the sky,
he blinked, then closed his eyes.
And in the distance, a stream of lights
ribboned sightless along the highway
on their way to nowhere much
as the last *gulamany* quietly died.

Stephen Yolland

A second on the cosmic calendar

Sky cracks open to reveal
more, and stories
about the sun's burn out
are premature, rumours
of the death of a righteous man.

But back to the sky. Birds
on the other side look
similar, but lack initiative
as if too long out of view
has led to complacency.
Something about wing tips raised
in nonchalance and beaks lowered
like the last night of *Mardi Gras*

has most observers packing up
field glasses and heading for home.
Like sky has folded in on itself
and the sun has finally got wise
to its own ontology.

Paul Mitchell

Acknowledgments

We gratefully acknowledge the following publications in which poems in this anthology first appeared.

p. xviii 'Ficus macrophylla' by Denise O'Hagan was first published in *The Beating Heart* (Ginninderra Press, 2020).

p. 5 'sanctity of shadows' (haiku) by Dianne Cikusa was published in *Cold Moon Journal*, December 2020.

p. 8 'At sea' by Anne Casey was published in *Plumwood Mountain*, Volume 6, No. 2: 'Intersecting Energies', August 2019.

p. 9 'Public health warning' by Piers Davies was published in *The Hobson.*

p. 11 'A Hill Outside Yanchep' by Alan Fyfe was published in *Westerly Magazine* 65, https://westerlymag.com.au/digital_archives/westerly-65-1/

p. 18 'The fall' by Jane Frank was published in her chapbook *Wide River* (Calanthe Press, 2020).

p. 24 'Wilderness, untouched' by Laura Jan Shore was published in her book *Water over Stone* (Interactive Press, 2011).

p. 26 'A pelican on Lake Eyre' by Gregory Piko was published in *Brushstrokes, Ros Spencer Poetry Contest Anthology 2016-19*, selected by Dennis Haskell and Rose van Son (WA Poets Publishing, 2019).

p. 29 'Summer ice' by Mark Mahemoff was published in his book *Urban Gleanings* (Ginninderra Press, 2017).

p. 38 'Response to the latest global warming statistics' by Paul Mitchell was published in his book, *Standard Variation* (Walleah Press, 2014).

p. 55 'Speaking to the narrative' by Arna Radovich was created using borrowed text from the South Australia, Murray-Darling Basin Royal Commission, *Report* (2019). In accordance with a Creative Commons Attribution 4.0 International Licence, random words and phrases were extracted, remixed and reconnected using additional text.

p. 56 '2035' by Angela Costi was published in *Otoliths*, Issue 59: Southern Spring, 2020.

p. 58 'Cassowaries, Etty Bay' by Jena Woodhouse was published in *Mascara Literary Review*, Issue 19, September 2016 and also in *The Disappearing*, Sydney (the Red Room Company).

p. 62 'All the beautiful outcasts' by Anne Casey was published in *Westerly Magazine,* The University of Western Australia, 19 March 2020.

p. 64 'One hundred flashing corellas' by Allan Padgett was published in *Letters To Our Home* (Follow That Cat, Subiaco WA, 2020).

p. 66 'Inter-wishing' by Caterina Mastroianni was published in 2021 at https://medium.com/resistance-poetry/inter-wishing-for-earth-635ca15f19c.

p. 68 'Failing to See regent honeyeaters at Springfield Lakes' by BR Dionysius was shortlisted in the 2019 MPU Poetry competition.

p. 76 'Spectacled flying-foxes' by Jena Woodhouse was published in *Australian Poetry Anthology* Vol. 7, 2019.

p. 78 'Dance of the river gums' by Gregory Piko was commended in the New Zealand Poetry Society's International Poetry Competition, 2020. It was also published in *Haumi ē! Hui ē! Tāiki ē! Stay Well Here*, the NZPS Poetry Anthology 2020, edited by Raewyn Alexander.

p. 80 'Survival', by John Bartlett, was published in *Songs of the Godforsaken* (Ginninderra Press, 2020) and won the 2020 Ada Cambridge Poetry Prize.

p. 82 '2049' by JV Birch was published in *Mslexia: Issue 84* (2019)

p. 84 'The Australian Anthropo-seen' by Michael J Leach was published in the What I Did Last Week: Online Exhibition Week 26, Creative Communities, City of Greater Bendigo.
https://www.bendigoregion.com.au/arts-culture-theatres/what-i-did-last-week-week-26

p. 85 'Birders' by Moya Pacey was published in *London Grip* September 2020 and in *Doggerland* (Recent Work Press, 2020).

p. 89 'Waitarmaroa Creek haiku' 3 and 4 by Piers Davies were published in *a fine line*.

p. 90 'DÉGUSTATION' by Nicole Rain Sellers won equal first place in the Society of Women Writers Tasmania Robyn Mathison Poetry Prize (2019) and was published in *Fossilised Lightning* (Girls on Key Poetry, 2021) by Nicole Rain Sellers and Rebecca Trowbridge.

p. 93 'Silky oak' by Vanessa Page was published in *Plumwood Mountain* 7.1 Plant Poetics, April 2020; on the *Stephen DiBiase Poetry Prize* website (2021) and in her chapbook *Botanical Skin* (Calanthe Press, 2021).

p. 95 'Brixton Street Wetlands' by Siobhan Hodge was published by *Right Now* on June 25, 2019.
https://rightnow.org.au/creative-works/brixton-street-wetlands/

p. 100 'Catch water. Hold fire.' by Claire Beynon was published when it was selected for the long-list in the 2020 Flash Frontier's Flash Fiction awards.

p. 104 'We of the Merri Merri are not a pathetic fallacy' by Dominique Hecq was published in *Meniscus*, Vol. 8, No. 1 2020, p. 100.
https://www.meniscus.org.au/Vol8Iss1.pdf

p. 106 'With words like doom-scrolling…' by Julie Maclean was published in *Plumwood Mountain*, 2020.

p.113 'I am not doing anything' by Ivy Ireland was published in *The Owl Inside* (Puncher and Wattmann, 2020).

p. 109 'Setting the rain free' by Geoff Callard was published in *Golden Walkman Magazine* Issue 6.2, Dialogue Submission Winner, 2018.

p. 124 'Enough rope to hang us all' by Linda Adair was published in her chapbook *The Unintended Consequences of the Shattering* (Melbourne Poets Union, 2020).

p. 126 'dad said' by Marilyn Humbert was published in *Earth Anthology* 2017 ed. Claire Everett.

p. 130 'Modern words' by Michael J Leach was published in *Otoliths*, Issue 60: Southern Summer, 2021.

p. 134 'Fishing' by Rachel Smith was published in *Catalyst* (New Zealand) 2017.

p. 138 'Unhooking the lip' by Sean West was first published in Red Room Poetry's *Writing Water* anthology.

p. 140 'Pillage' by Shaine Melrose was published in the Friendly Street Poets Goolwa Anthology 1, *Fleurieu Flow*, 2019.

p. 142 'Night vision' by Stacey Cotter Manière was published in its unabridged form in *The Lissome Magazine Rewilding*, Edition 2.

p. 144 'Survivalist' by Penelope Layland was published in *Rochford Street Review*, 2019.

p. 151 'Waxing moon in Virgo' by Ivy Ireland was published in *Porch Light* (Puncher and Wattmann, 2015).

p. 155 'In the next galaxy' by Laura Jan Shore was published in *Verdant Truth Serum*, Vol. 5, 2019.

p. 160 'departures, arrivals' by Stu Hatton was published as earlier versions in *Overland* no. 215, 2014, and *Glitching* (Outer Publishing, 2014).

p. 168 'The days' by Gail Hennessy received a 'Special Mention' and was published online by the Hunter Writers Centre in response to their Pen-demic competition, February 2021.

p. 169 'Afterlife' by Jane Frank was published in *Verity La*, 2019, and in her chapbook *Wide River* (Calanthe Press, 2020).

p. 170 'design' by Ivy Ireland was published in *Porch Light* (Puncher and Wattmann, 2015).

p. 172 'Prohoros—in the Cave of the Apocalypse' by Jena Woodhouse was published in *Antipodes*, the journal of the Greek-Australian Cultural League, Melbourne, No. 58, 2012.

p. 174 '240 grams; by John Bennett was published in *Planet in Peril: An anthology for our time*, Ed., Isabelle Kenyon, (Fly on the Wall Press, 2019).

p. 176 'O let them be left, wildness and wet—' by Julie Maclean was published in *Stilts,* 2020.

p. 178 'A climate of mortality meets Melbourne winter' by Anne Elvey was published in *Transnational Literature* 10, No. 2, May 2018.

p. 183 'Cliff' by Rachel J Fenton was first published in *The Rialto* issue 86, 2016. ISSN 02685981

p. 188 'The Revelation myth' by Lincoln Jaques was published in *Oscen Magazine*, ed. Janna Tay, November 2020.

p. 190 'Before our Earth falls silent' by Margaret Bradstock was published in *Brief Garden* (Puncher & Wattmann, 2019).

p. 191 'Double rainbow' by Mark Mahemoff was published in his book *Urban Gleanings* (Ginninderra Press, 2017).

p. 192 'This weight I hold' by Michelle Brock was published in keep or kill (*Eucalypt 29*, 2020) old-growth forest (*Poems From Today's World),* Red Moon 2020), Mars-tinged moon (*Moonbathing* 23, 2020), and she runs to me (*Eucalypt 27*, 2019).

p. 194 'Decline' by Marilyn Humbert was published in *Atlas Poetica 38*, 2019.

p. 209 'Tabula rasa' by Penelope Layland was published in *Not Very Quiet,* Issue 5, 21 September 2019.

Biographies

Adele Ogiér Jones is from Melbourne and works internationally. With four collections of poetry, including *Counting the Chiperoni* (Ginninderra Press, 2019), she is published in anthologies and e-journals including *The Blue Nib, Burrow* and *Messages from the Embers* (Black Quill Press, 2020)

Alan Fyfe is a poet from Mandurah whose work has featured in *Westerly, Overland,* and *Cottonmouth.* He is a winner of the Karl Popper Philosophy Award, and his first novel was shortlisted for the TAG Hungerford Award and the CP Aware Prize.

Alexandra Fraser is an Auckland poet. She has published two collections of poetry, *Star Trails* (2019) and *Conversations by Owl-light* (Steele Roberts Aotearoa, 2014). Her work is also published in many New Zealand and overseas magazines and anthologies. She is still trying to finish writing a pair of YA fantasies.

Alicia Sometimes is a writer and broadcaster. She has performed her spoken word and poetry at many venues, festivals and events around the world. She is director and co-writer of the art/science planetarium shows, *Elemental* and *Particle/Wave.* Her TedxUQ talk in 2019 was about the passion of combining art with science.

Allan Lake, originally from Saskatchewan, has lived in Vancouver, Cape Breton, Ibiza, Tasmania and Melbourne. Poetry Collection: *Sand in the Sole* (Xlibris, 2014). Lake won Lost Tower Publications (UK) Comp 2017, Melbourne Spoken Word Poetry Fest 2018 and publication in New Philosopher 2020. His latest chapbook is *My Photos of Sicily* (Ginninderra Press, 2020).

Allan Padgett is a Western Australian poet, published in a range of journals. He holds a deep and abiding interest in the power of poetry to entertain and to positively assist in transforming our world for the better. Allan's first book, *Lumbering Towards Infinity*, was published in May 2021.

Amanda Anastasi is a Melbourne poet and recipient of the Wheeler Centre Hot Desk Fellowship, the Ada Cambridge Poetry Prize and Words in Winter Trentham Poetry Prize. She is currently Poet in Residence at the Monash Climate Change Communication Research Hub. Her poetry collection is *The Inheritors* (Black Pepper, 2021).

Dr Andrew Hingston is an ecologist and author of 37 peer-reviewed research papers, covering topics such as pollination systems, invasive species, swift parrots, and the responses of birds to logging and wildfire. He currently works as a wildlife guide for Inala Nature Tours, and as Project Manager for the Inala Foundation.

Andrew Geoffrey Kwabena Moss is an Anglo-Ghanaian writer/teacher, living in Australia. He explores liminal landscapes, identity and constructs of race. Featured in several journals and anthologies including *The Best New British and Irish Poets Anthology 2019-2021* published by The Black Spring Press Group. They will also publish his forthcoming debut poetry collection.

Angela Costi's recent poetry collection is *An Embroidery of Old Maps and New*. City of Melbourne funding is supporting her to work on a new poetry manuscript: *The Heart of the Advocate*. Current issues of *Meniscus Literary Journal, Teesta Review, Westerly, Cordite* and *Rochford Street Review* include her poetry and reviews.

Ann Shenfield has worked as an animation filmmaker, illustrator and writer. Her animated films have received prizes including selection to the Official Competition at the Berlin Film Festival. Her poetry has received prizes, including the Judith Wright Poetry Award for her collection *You Can Get Only So Close on Google Earth* (Arcadia, 2010).

Anne Casey is an award-winning Irish poet/writer and scholarship PhD researcher living in Australia. A journalist, magazine editor, legal author and media communications director for 30 years, Anne is author of three collections, with a fourth book forthcoming in 2021. Her work is widely published internationally, ranking in *The Irish Times'* Most Read. anne-casey.com @1annecasey

Anne Elvey is a poet, editor and researcher, living on Boonwurrung (Bunurong) Country in bayside Melbourne (Naarm). Her most recent poetry publication is *Obligations of Voice* (Recent Work Press 2021). As Managing Editor of *Plumwood Mountain* journal (2014–2020), she edited *hope for whole: poets speak up to Adani* (2018).

Annie Hill Otness is an award-winning author, playwright, poet, artist and environmental activist. Her journey is one of survival on trackless voyages where few have ventured. Her works include *Dream Beaches Invisible Landscapes* (2017), *The Vision Books* (as M.A. Hill), and *The Travellers* trilogy.
http://annieotness.blogspot.com or www.ozartworks.com

AR Levett B.A, B.Comm.(Hons) is an award-winning, emerging WA author. His Story Mentoring services help writers hone their skills and stories. He has taught at ECU and for the WA writing community and served on the KSP BoM. He is writing a speculative-fiction series. www.thestorymentor.com.au www.arlevett.weebly.com

Arna Radovich writes for both adults and children and across genre and form. Her work has been published in anthologies, literary journals, and magazines, most recently in *Verity La*, *Meniscus* and *ZineWest*. She won the *ZineWest* 2020 Writing Award for her poem, 'Last Breath' and lives in the Blue Mountains.

BR Dionysius is based in Queensland, Australia. He has published four collections of poetry, two chapbooks, an artist's book and a verse novel. He has lived in Melbourne, Brisbane and Ipswich. He is an English teacher, was founding Director of the Queensland Poetry Festival and in his spare time watches birds.

Carl Walsh lives and writes on Wurundjeri land. He's a poet, crossword compiler, lexicographer of fictional words, writer of horoscopes and other fairy stories. His poetry has been published in journals including *StylusLit, Rabbit, Wales Haiku Journal, Cordite, Southerly, Meanjin, Plumwood Mountain, Australian Poetry Journal, Verity La* and *Tokyo Poetry Journal.*

Caterina Mastroianni lives in Sydney, Australia. She has published poetry in print literary magazines and anthologies. A complete list of publications are listed on the AustLit website. Since then, she has returned to her creative roots by publishing poems online on the Medium platform. This has encouraged her to continue with her creative pursuits.

Claire Albrecht is a Newcastle-based poet and researcher. She was the 2019 Emerging Writers Festival fellow at the State Library of Victoria, a 2020 Varuna 'Writing Fire, Writing Drought' fellow, and will be a resident at the Helene Wurlitzer Foundation, New Mexico in 2021. Prizes for her work include the Karen Thrift Poetry Prize in 2020.

Claire Beynon is a Dunedin-based artist and published writer with a steady history of exhibitions and awards. In addition to her solo practice, she works collaboratively on a diverse range of interdisciplinary projects with fellow artists, writers, scientists and musicians in New Zealand and abroad. She has a special affection for foraminifera, fungi, ice and prime numbers. www.clairebeynon.com

Colleen Z Burke's most recent and twelfth poetry collection is *Sculpting a landscape,* 2019. She has also published two memoirs, *The Waves Turn* and *The Human Heart is a Bold Traveller*, and is co-editor of the anthology *The Turning Wave: Poems and Songs of Irish Australia.*

David Brooks' latest work is a collection of essays, *Animal Dreams* (Sydney University Press, 2021). He is the author of several acclaimed collections of poetry, the most recent *Open House* (University of Queensland Press, 2015).

Dianne Cikusa has published in several literary journals and anthologies. She is the author of three poetry books, including a bilingual collection which received First Prize in Poetry in the 2020 Global Ebook Awards. She has produced three print books of wisdom quotes, and an Ebook Series due for release (2021).

Dominique Hecq is a Belgian-born poet living in Melbourne. She writes across genres and sometimes across tongues. Her works include a novel, three collections of short stories and eleven books of poetry including *Tracks* (2020) and *Songlines* (2021). With Eugen Bacon, she also co-authored *Speculate* (2021), a microlit selection.

Edna Heled lives in New Zealand. An artist, art therapist, counsellor and travel journalist, her writing includes short stories, poetry and non-fiction. She has published in *NZ Herald, Short and Twisted, Flash Frontier, Fresh Ink, Backstory Australia, Landing Press, Poetry NZ Year Book 2021*, and more.

Elspeth Findlay dwells in the Northern Rivers of NSW. She has poetry and prose published in the *Northerly, Emergent Literary Journal, Furiously Knocking* and *Journey* anthologies and touring with the Bimblebox 153 Birds exhibition. Elspeth is studying Arts, majoring in Creative Writing at SCU.

Emily Mitchell is a poet, writer and researcher, and lives with her husband and two children on Awabakal country in Newcastle, NSW. She has worked with communities in Indonesia and Papua New Guinea documenting threats of environmental damage, and is passionate about the connection between people and the environment, and their Creator.

Gail Hennessy has been published widely in newspapers, literary supplements, journals and anthologies. Her poetry has won a number of local and national prizes. Her published work includes *Witnessing* (self-published, 2010), *Written on Water* (Flying Island Books, 2017) and *The M Word* (Girls on Key, 2019).

Gail Ingram is award-winning writer and author of *Contents Under Pressure* (Pūkeko Publications, 2019). Her work appears in *Landfall, Poetry New Zealand, Cordite, The Blue Nib* and others. She is editor for *a fine line* (NZ Poetry Society), a poetry editor for *takahē*, and teaches at *Write On* in Christchurch, Aotearoa.
https://www.theseventhletter.nz/

Garry Dean is an Australian short story writer, and sometimes poet, who harbors secret and dubious ambitions of one day writing a novel. His work has appeared in numerous online magazines and print anthologies. He won the 2020 Dickinson Award for blind and vision impaired writers. www.garrydean.wordpress.com

Geoff Callard is a New Zealand-born, Melbourne-based writer. He has had poetry published in numerous journals across the globe and in a number of anthologies including *Planet in Peril* and the Australian bushfires anthology—*Messages from the Embers*. He won the Gideon Poetry Prize Winter 2020 and has a chapbook planned for publication in August 2021 with Kelsay Books.

Gillian Swain's first poetry collection is *My Skin its own Sky* (Flying Islands Press, 2019) and her work is included in various anthologies and journals. Gillian shared first place with Magdalena Ball in the MacLean's Booksellers Award (Grieve Project 2019) and is the Co-Director and poetry curator for 'IF Maitland' Indie Writers Festival.

Gregory Piko's writing has appeared in *Westerly, Authora Australis, Communion Arts Journal*, the *Canberra Times*, *Poetry d'Amour*, *StylusLit*, *Verity La, Shot Glass Journal* and the *Australian Poetry Anthology* among other places. His collection, *breaking my journey*, is published by *Red Moon Press*. Please visit www.gregorypiko.com.

Helen Anderson is a New Zealand-based poet, academic and researcher. She is a past winner of the Auckland War Memorial Museum 'Lest We Forget' Poetry Competition and recently published online in *The Blue Nib* (2020) and *Milly Magazine* (2020).

Helena Baird is a scientist with a PhD in ecology; studying the natural world is her profession, but exploring nature with poetry is her love. She has published on nature conservation for travel magazines and academic journals, with several poems emerging in anthologies this year. Having previously worked in Antarctica and Indonesia, she now resides in Melbourne.

Ian Reid grew up in New Zealand and now lives in Australia. The most recent of his 15 books is a novel, *The Madwoman's Coat.* His poetry and other work has been widely published in several countries, winning awards (e.g. the Antipodes prize) and being translated into five languages.

Ivy Ireland is the author of *Incidental Complications* (2007), *Porch Light* (2015) and *The Owl Inside* (2020). Ivy holds a PhD in Creative Writing at the University of Newcastle; her literary awards include the Australian Young Poet Fellowship, the Harri Jones Memorial Prize, the Thunderbolt Prize, and the Newcastle Poetry Prize.

Jane Frank is originally from the Fraser Coast but now based in Brisbane where she lectures at Griffith University. Her most recent chapbook is *Wide River* (Calanthe Press, 2020). Her work has twice been shortlisted for the Thomas Shapcott Poetry Prize. Most recently, her poems have appeared in *Westerly, Live Encounters, Antipodes, Shearsman*, *StylusLit* and *Not Very Quiet.*

Jason Richardson explores landscapes through various media. The Soundscapes exhibition at Wagga Wagga Art Gallery in 2020 showcased his multidisciplinary art, including musical videos incorporating Riverina locations. His book *Earthwords* merged the haiku tradition with the Dadaist cut-up technique for an exhibition at Griffith Regional Art Gallery in 2019.

Jena Woodhouse has eleven book and chapbook publications across various genres, including six poetry titles, most recently *News from the Village: Travels in Rural Greece* (Picaro Poets, 2021). In 2021, her poems appear in *Live Encounters* (US), *The Galway Review* (Ireland), *Antipodes: A Global Journal* (US); *Not Very Quiet*; the *Montreal Poetry Prize Anthology 2020*; *Authora Australis*; *StylusLit*; and *foam:e.*

Jennifer Allen is a Melbourne based poet, whose first collection of poems, *The Cut Worm,* was published by Precious Press. Jennifer has two young daughters, Josephine and Eleni, who inspire her with their wit, compassion and creativity.

John Bartlett is the author of eight books of fiction, non-fiction and poetry. In 2019, his first chapbook, *The Arms of Men* was published (MPU) and *Songs of the Godforsaken* followed in June 2020 (Picaro Poets). *Awake at 3am*, his full collection, was released in 2020 (Ginninderra Press). John also reviews and podcasts at beyondtheestuary.com

John Bennett After working for NSW National Parks & Wildlife, he gained a PhD on poetics, worked for a while as a university lecturer then taught ecological thought in community settings in Sydney, and on the Mid-North Coast. He was Artistic Director of the Bellingen Readers and Writers Festival for five years. frogdownstairs@gmail.com; photovoltaicpoetry.com.au

John Robert Grogan is an Irish-Australian poet living in Sydney, Australia. Childhood life in Ireland's Wicklow mountains, time in the Mediterranean, and his Australian wanderings cultivated a curiosity and love for the natural world and the connectivity of all things. He is published in *Live Encounters Poetry and Writing* and *The Blue Nib.*

Josie/Jocelyn Deane is a student at the university of Melbourne. Their work has appeared in *Cordite, Australian Poetry* and *Overland,* among others. In 2021 they were one of the recipients of the Queensland Poetry Festival Ekphrasis award. They live on unceded Wurundjeri land.

Joy Reid has appeared in *Coppertales, The Australian Writers' Journal, Poetrix, New England Review, Muse* and *LiNQ* in Australia and numerous international literary magazines and zines.

Julie Maclean's poetry, fiction and reviews have appeared in *The Best Australian Poetry, Cordite Review, The Griffith Review, Island, Overland, Poetry* and *Southerly*. She is the author of five poetry collections. *When I Saw Jimi*, shortlisted for The Crashaw Prize (Salt) was joint winner of the Geoff Stevens Memorial Poetry Prize (Indigo Dreams Publishing, UK). www.juliemacleanwriter.com

JV Birch lives in Adelaide. Her poems have been anthologised, exhibited and published in Australia, the UK, Canada and the US. She has three chapbooks with Ginninderra Press and a full-length collection, *more than here*. Visit www.jvbirch.com for more information.

Kate Nicholas Edgar chose to write the poem 'Tales of old' because she is concerned about what future on Earth will be like and hopes it won't end in catastrophe. The poem finishes on a note of optimism as she believes that Earth can recover if we make a change.

Kelly Van Nelson is the #1 bestselling author of *Graffiti Lane, Retrospective*, and *Punch and Judy* poetry collections. She is a KSP First Edition Fellowship recipient, AusMumpreneur 'Big Idea Changing the World', Roar Success Best Book and Most Powerful Influencer gold award winner, represented by The Newman Agency www.kellyvannelson.com.

Laura Jan Shore teaches poetry in northern NSW. She won the *Martha Richardson Poetry Prize* (2012) and the FAW John Shaw Nielson *Award* (2009). Her poetry collections include *Breathworks* (Dangerously Poetic Press, 2002), *Water over Stone* (Interactive Press, 2011), and *Afterglow* (Interactive Press, 2020). Her work appears in literary journals across four continents.

Leigh Roswen is a writer and amateur naturalist from Wollongong, NSW. She maintains a blog dedicated to nature writing and photography. Currently she's engrossed in a project to describe all the visible insects in her backyard. Leigh has had success in short fiction markets and competitions with her creative writing.

Les Wicks has toured widely and seen publication in over 400 different magazines, anthologies and newspapers across 32 countries in 15 languages. His 14th book of poetry is *Belief* (Flying Islands, 2019).
http://leswicks.tripod.com/lw.htm

Lincoln Jaques' poetry, fiction and travel writing has appeared in *Tough Magazine, Noir Nation, Mother Mary Comes to Me: A Pop Culture Poetry Anthology, The Blue Nib, Mayhem, Poetry NZ Yearbook* and *Blackmail Press.* He was a finalist in the 2018 NZ Emerging Poets. He lives in Auckland.

Linda Adair is a poet and editor of Rochford Press/*Rochford Street Review.* MPU published her book *The Unintended Consequences of the Shattering* in 2020. She has been published in *25 Miles from Here Pure Slush Vol 21, Messages from the Embers* (Black Quill Press, 2020), *To End All Wars* (Puncher & Wattmann, 2018) and various journals.

Linda Stevenson is a poet/painter living in Frankston, Victoria. Her poetry has been published in recent years in a variety of literary journals, both online and in print. Linda's work often highlights environmental and social conscience themes.

Lorne Johnson lives in Newtown, Sydney and teaches at Ascham School. He is a fan of punk rock, Jim Jarmusch, classic American cars, good coffee, meditation, bushwalking and birding. His poetry has been published widely. Pitt Street Poetry released *Morton* in 2016. He misses Uluru and Kata Tjuta.

Lorraine Gibson is a retired anthropologist, painter and poet. Her work is published internationally in books, journals, anthologies and magazines and includes her book *We Don't Do Dots: Aboriginal Art and Culture in Wilcannia, New South Wales.*

Louise Hopewell is a Melbourne-based haiku poet, playwright and songwriter. Louise won the inaugural John Bird Dreaming Award for Haiku in 2021, as well as the H Gene Murtha Memorial Senryu Contest in 2020. When not writing, Louise can be found riding her bicycle, playing ukulele or camping under snow gums.

Magdalena Ball is a novelist, poet, reviewer and interviewer, and is Managing Editor of *Compulsive Reader.* She has been widely published in literary journals, anthologies and online, and is the author of several published books of poetry and fiction including, most recently, *Unreliable Narratives* (Girls on Key Press, 2019).

Margaret Bradstock has eight published collections of poetry, including *The Pomelo Tree* (winner of the Wesley Michel Wright Prize) and *Barnacle Rock* (winner of the Woollahra Festival Award, 2014). Editor of *Antipodes* (2011) and *Caring for Country* (2017), Margaret won the Banjo Paterson Poetry Award in 2014, 2015 and 2017. Her latest collection, from Puncher & Wattmann, is *Brief Garden* (2019).

Margaret Owen Ruckert is an award-winning poet, whose works are widely published. Her latest book *Sky on Sea* is a collection of tanka on Sydney's waterways and beaches. She presents regular writing workshops as Facilitator of Hurstville's Discovery Writers and convenes a local Café Poets group.

Marilyn Humbert lives in Sydney NSW Australia. Her tanka and haiku appear in international and Australian journals, anthologies and online. Her free verse poems have been awarded prizes in competitions, published online, in anthologies and journals most recently in *FemAsia Magazine* and *Live Encounters Poetry & Writing*, July 2021.

Mark Mahemoff is an Australian poet, critic and psychotherapist. He has published four books of poetry and a CD anthology of his work. His work is represented in magazines and anthologies internationally. His next book of poetry is due for publication by Puncher & Wattmann in 2021.

Mark Roberts is a writer, critic and publisher living on Darug and Gundungurra country. He is a co-editor of *Rochford Street Review* and his latest collection, *Concrete Flamingos,* was published by Island Press in 2016.

Matina Doumos is now a resident of Athens, Greece, where she works in organic certification. She is passionate about poetry and soil regeneration. Recently her poems and translations have been published in *Hecate Journal, Southerly, Antipodes (a Global Journal of Australian/New Zealand Literature), Antipodes (Journal of the Greek Australian Cultural League)* & the online journal *Live Encounters.*

Matt Hetherington is a writer, music-maker, teacher, and moderate self-promoter based in northern New South Wales. He has been writing poetry for over 30 years, and his sixth collection, *Kaleidoscopes,* was published by Recent Work Press in September 2020. www.matthetherington.net

Michael J Leach lives on unceded Dja Dja Wurrung Country and works as a senior lecturer at Monash University School of Rural Health. His poems reside in *Rabbit*, *Cordite*, *Meniscus*, *Plumwood Mountain*, *NatureVolve*, the *2021 Hippocrates Prize Anthology*, and elsewhere. Michael's debut poetry collection is *Chronicity* (Melbourne Poets Union, 2020).

Michelle Brock is a Queanbeyan short story writer and poet. She loves experimenting with Japanese forms and her tanka prose, poems and haiga appear regularly in Australian and overseas journals. Her recent publications include *Ebb and Flow*, an anthology by Friday Writers, 2018.

Moya Costello has two collections of short creative prose and two short novels (*Kites in Jakarta, Small Ecstasies; The Office as a Boat, Harriet Chandler*), and critical and creative writing in journals and anthologies. She is adjunct lecturer, Southern Cross University, writing these prose poems with specimens in the Herbarium.

Moya Pacey lives in Canberra, Australia. Her third collection, *Doggerland*, was published by Recent Work Press, October 2020. https://recentworkpress.com/books/product/doggerland/
She co-edits the online journal, *Not Very Quiet* notveryquiet.com.
https://www.facebook.com/Moya-Pacey-Poet-162226857195634/?ref=settings

Nicole Rain Sellers' poems appear in books and journals including *Fossilised Lightning* (Girls on Key Poetry, 2021), *Plumwood Mountain, The Enchanting Verses, Heroic Fantasy Quarterly, The Blue Nib, Burrow, Australian Poetry Collaboration*, and *TEXT*. Her writing has been awarded in the Robyn Mathison, Alice Sinclair, Sydney Hammond, and other competitions. www.nicolerainsellers.com

Pat Simmons lives at Scarborough on the NSW south coast. She's a writer of poetry, short stories, flash fiction and children's picture books. Her poems have been published in School Magazine and also included in a number of anthologies. Details of her published picture books can be found on her website. www.patsimmonswriter.com.au

Paul Mitchell is a Melbourne-based writer. His latest book is *Matters of Life and Faith* (Coventry Press, 2021), a collection of personal essays. His most recent poetry collection, *Standard Variation* (Walleah Press, 2016), was short-listed for the Adelaide Festival Awards for Literature John Bray Poetry Prize.

Penelope Layland's most recent book is *Nigh* (Recent Work Press, 2020). Her 2018 book, *Things I've thought to tell you since I saw you last* (Recent Work Press), was shortlisted for the Kenneth Slessor Prize and the ACT Book of the Year and won an ACT Writing and Publishing Award.

Peter Ramm is a poet who writes on Gundungarra lands of NSW. He has recently published poems with *Cordite, Westerly*, and *Plumwood Mountain*. In 2020-21 Peter won the Harri Jones Memorial Prize and the South Coast Writer's Centre Poetry Award, and was shortlisted in the Blake and Newcastle Poetry Prizes.

Phillip Hall lives in Melbourne. His publications include *Borroloola Class* (IPSI, 2018), *Fume* (UWAP, 2018) and (as editor) *Diwurruwurru: Poetry from the Gulf of Carpentaria* (Blank Rune Press, 2015). He also publishes the e-journal *Burrow*: https://oldwaterratpublishing.com. His collection entitled *Cactus*, was published by Recent Work Press in 2021.

Piers Davies was born in Sydney lived mainly in Auckland/Tamaki Makaurau. Long-time poet published extensively in New Zealand/ Aotearoa and overseas. Co-coordinator of Titirangi Poets and co-editor of Titirangi Poets Ezines. Scriptwriter with Peter Weir of feature films *Homesdale* and *The Cars That Ate Paris.*

Rachel J Fenton's poetry has appeared in *English, Overland, Landfall, The Rialto*, and *Magma*, and her chapbook *Beerstorming with Charlotte Brontë in New York* is published by Ethel Zine and Micro Press.

Rachel Smith is a writer of poetry and short fiction. Her work has been published in journals and anthologies in Aotearoa New Zealand and overseas including Best Small Fictions 2020 and Best Microfiction 2019. She is an editor at *Flash Frontier.*
@rachelmsmithnz1 http://rachelmsmithnz.wix.com/rachel-smith

Rebecca Douglas is an Adelaide-based writer whose work has been published by *Overland, The Sydney Morning Herald, The Guardian, Kill Your Darlings, Visible Ink, Verandah, The Big Issue, ABC The Drum*, and various other lovely places.

Rebecca Trowbridge has spent time as an army corporal, geologist, market research caller, ski lodge manager, high school teacher and university tutor, while living and working around Australia. Her latest eco-poetry volume *Fossilised Lightning*, co-authored with Nicole Rain Sellers, is available from publisher Girls on Key.
rebeccatrowbridge.com

Robert J Conlon has been writing for more than twenty-five years. Published in literary magazines, journals, blogs and magazines, he made the Victorian slam final twice, in 2011 and 2012. He is presently the full-time carer of his mother and rides a Triumph motorcycle.

Robyn Sykes is published in journals and anthologies nationally, internationally and online. Nature, human behaviour and a BSc (Hons) inform her work. Recently, her poem 'Forest Tracks' appeared in bushfire anthology *Messages from the Embers: From Devastation to Hope* (Black Quill Press, 2020). Robyn coordinates A Brush with Poetry in Binalong, near Canberra.

Rosanna E Licari's work has recently appeared in *fourW: New Writing, Shearsman, TEXT, Well-known corners—Poetry on the Move* (Canberra Uni), *Lane Cove Literary Awards 2019 anthology* (2020), *Anthology of Australian Prose Poetry* (MUP, 2020), *Scars: an anthology of microlit* (Spineless Wonders, 2020) and *Pulped Fiction: an anthology of microlit* (Spineless Wonders, 2021).

Ruth Nelson is a clinical psychologist and sometimes writer who wonders how to use those skills in service of climate justice. She hosted the Creating Space Project podcast and is on the editorial team of *The Activist Practitioner*. She is also a spokesperson for the Climate Media Centre and lives on Gadigal land.

Sally Denshire is an Anglo-Australian poet based in Albury-Wodonga on Wiradjuri land. Her PhD from the University of Technology, Sydney, was autoethnographic. She is published in *fourW* New Writing (2016, 2017, 2018, 2019), *Not Very Quiet, realtime* and *Plumwood Mountain.*

Sandra Renew's poetry collections are *It's the sugar, Sugar,* Recent Work Press, 2021 and *Acting Like a Girl,* Recent Work Press, 2019 (winner 2020 ACT Writing and Publishing Award for Poetry and shortlisted for the 2020 ACT Book of the Year). Her tanka and microlit pieces are published nationally and internationally.

Sean West is a Meanjin-based poet, disability support worker, and workshop facilitator. He received an Arts Queensland Individuals Fund grant in 2021 and was shortlisted for the Thomas Shapcott Poetry Prize in 2020 and 2019. He is the founding editor of *Blue Bottle Journal.* Find him at www.callmemariah.com.

Shaine Melrose has had poems published in *Friendly Street Poets* anthologies, *The Crow, Indaily, The Mozzie, Raining Poetry in Adelaide* and *Tamba.* She was highly commended in Adelaide Plains Poetry Competition 2020, a finalist in the 2019 Goolwa Poetry Cup and runner-up in 2018, also a finalist in the 2019 South Australian Summer Slam.

Siobhan Hodge has a PhD in English literature. She won the 2017 Kalang Eco-Poetry Award and was shortlisted for the 2019 Fair Australia Prize. Her work has been published in several places, including *Rabbit, Peril. Overland, Westerly, Southerly,* and *Cordite.* Her chapbook, *Justice for Romeo,* is available through Cordite Books.

Stacey Cotter Manière is a Poet and Creative Director based in Sydney. Her poetry features in *SMEAR: Poems for Girls,* published by Andrew McMeel and various international magazines. She appears in *The Alphabet of Women*, to be released as an anthology by Ginninderra Press in 2021. Follow on Instagram @stace.c.m

Stephen 'Yolly' Yolland has been a writer for over 30 years, responsible for some of Australia's best-known ad campaigns. One volume of poetry is released (available from Amazon) called *Read Me.* He has also been a finalist in Australian and overseas short story competitions, a creative medium he especially enjoys.

Stu Hatton lives and writes on unceded Dja Dja Wurrung country in Campbells Creek, Victoria. Recently his work has appeared in *Verity La* and *Burrow.* He is currently preparing his third poetry collection, entitled *In the Not-too-distant Present.*

Sunny Wignall lives on Whadjuk Nyoongar Boodja. He writes to stand with, hope, rage, and remember. His poetry is published in the anthology B*ecoming Known: Emerging Poets* 2020, *Poetry d'Amour* 2015, ekphrastic poetry anthology *Creative Connections* 2015, online journal *Recoil* and a chapbook *These Reeds.*

Vanessa Page is a Queensland poet. She has published five collections of poetry, including *Confessional Box* (Walleah Press) which was the winner of the 2013 Anne Elder Award. A new collection of poems *Botanical Skin* (Calanthe Press) was published in July 2021. Vanessa blogs at vanessapage.wordpress.com

Viki Mealings is a poet, musician, songwriter, and artist. In 2015 her reworking of W B Yeats' *The Ballad of Moll Magee* was featured in Art Saves Lives International which is an online art magazine based in Portsmouth, UK. Her poetry explores issues of inequality and alienation and she has recently released a poetry collection entitled *Her Poetic Body.*

About the Australian Conservation Foundation

Right now, a pollution and extinction crisis threatens our living world. Climate damage and habitat destruction are our biggest challenges.

We're living with the consequences of bad decisions, discredited ideas and short-term thinking. The big polluters. The rigged rules. The politicians who forget they represent the people.

But we don't accept the story; we must sacrifice nature for a quick buck. People made this crisis and together we can solve it.

The Australian Conservation Foundation is Australia's national environmental organisation. We are more than 700,000 people who speak out for the air we breathe, the water we drink, and the places and wildlife we love. We are proudly independent, non-partisan and funded by donations from our community.

By purchasing *Poetry for the Planet* today, you will help to ensure our air, water and soil remain healthy for future generations.

All profits will be donated to the Australian Conservation Foundation. Thank you.

To find out more about the ACF and its programs, please visit the website acf.org.au.

CPSIA information can be obtained
at www.ICGtesting.com
Printed in the USA
LVHW031639271121
704627LV00004B/222

9 780645 114577